The Making of Ministry

Timothy F. Sedgwick

D1512243

COWLEY PUBLICATIONS
Cambridge ✦ *Boston*
Massachusetts

Published in the United States of America by Cowley Publications, a division
of the Society of St. John the Evangelist. No portion of this book may be re-
produced, stored in or introduced into a retrieval system, or transmitted, in
any form or by any means—including photocopying—without the prior
written permission of Cowley Publications, except in the case of brief quotations embodied in critical articles and reviews.

International Standard Book Number: 1-56101-082-0
Library of Congress Number: 93-22815

Library of Congress Cataloging-in-Publication Data
Sedgwick, Timothy F.
  The Making of Ministry/Timothy F. Sedgwick
    p. cm.
  Includes bibliographical references.
  ISBN 1-56101-082-0
    1. Episcopal Church.   2. Church.   3. Clergy—Office.   4. Anglican
Communion.   I. Title.
BX5930.2.S43 1993
283'.73—dc20   93-22815

Biblical quotations are from the *New Revised Standard Version* (New York:
Oxford University Press, 1989.)

This book is printed on acid-free paper and was produced in the United
States of America.

Cover illustration is taken from the stained glass window "Feed My Sheep,"
located in Streatham.

Cowley Publications
28 Temple Place
Boston, Massachusetts 02111

To
Wes Frensdorff
and
Rachel Hosmer

"Encouraged by their examples,
aided by their prayers, and strengthened
by their fellowship...."

Preface

The change in the relationship between the church and the contemporary world is as fundamental and radical as the change brought about in the fourth century with the establishment of the Christian church as the state religion of the Roman Empire. In the United States, the religious establishment was abolished with the separation of church and state, but American Christians are only beginning to confront the challenge of becoming the church in a secular world. Meeting this challenge requires rethinking the whole life of the church—from baptismal initiation and faith formation to mission and ministry. Therefore the chapters of this book address the question of Christian identity and how the church should order its life in this new missionary context.

On the basis of a sacramental understanding of Christian faith, I focus on ordained ministry and the development of leadership for the church, clergy ethics and the purposes of ministry, and how the church should teach what faith means and demands. As practical studies, each chapter may also be read separately and then used either as background material or as a focus for discussing particular issues.

The primary source for the reflections developed here are conversations about broad matters of Christian faith and vocation and about particular, political issues in the life of the church. No one has been more important in these conversations than the seminarians here at Seabury-Western, while the regular conversations of fellow faculty—often in addressing matters of our common life—inform my thinking more than I know. I am equally grateful to the wide range of people in the church with whom I have had the opportunity to share in reflecting upon the life of the church. Examples and specific insights that I have offered in this book are often drawn from those conversations. I thank all those who have had sufficient trust to invite me to share in their work, provided hospitality, and offered their own assessments and visions of what the church is called to become.

Finally, I am grateful to Seabury-Western Theological Seminary for providing an extended sabbatical that made possible the timely completion of this manuscript, to the Conant Fund of the Episcopal Church, and to Cynthia Shattuck for her editorial wisdom and labors.

Table of Contents

1

Mistaken Identities

In the seminary classroom and in teaching educational events for clergy and laity, I emphasize that Anglicans understand Christian faith as a matter of holiness, as a way of life that reflects and deepens our relationship with God. How then, I ask, is God present in our lives, in our primary relations at home and in the community, in our work, in the crises of life, and in our dying? In turn, how do we respond, and what do we do, in order to acknowledge and deepen our sense of the presence of God? What disciplines form us in faith?

Clergy and lay leaders say that such questions about Christian faith and Christian life are difficult to address. Few people associate church with the meaning of the Greek word for the church, *ekklesia*, a word that literally means a gathering or assembly. Instead, the word "church" is associated with a building and with Sunday worship, since most people in the church come to worship on Sunday. Yet in the church at large there are an increasing number of conferences on lay ministry, gift discernment for ministry, catechumenate programs, and opportunities for ministry in outreach programs, whether they are pastoral visitation programs or opportunities to work at food pantries and homeless shelters. There are also those who gather to address their lives as Christians in the world, for example in the workplace or in the family. Still, such opportunities involve relatively small numbers of people and always are in tension with the time and energy concentrated inward on the maintenance of the church. As one woman commented, "I only have so much time. I would like to be part of more discussions and education events, but I am on the stewardship committee. That takes all the time I've got."

There are two sides to the church. One side is expressed in the vitality that offers new and constructive opportunities for growth; the other is expressed in a narrow preoccupation with the life of the church and its maintenance. This two-sidedness exists because the church is what sociologists call a voluntary association.[1] That is to say, the church is formed by people who choose to belong to it. Since these people associate with the church because they want to, churches have groups of highly committed persons who may begin new ventures. On the other hand, those committed to the church and assuming leadership in the church easily become preoccupied with the church's survival, and how it can attract and keep new members. This in turn leads the church to appeal to and so reflect the cultural beliefs and attitudes of the people it seeks to attract.

The dynamics that lead to the assimilation of the church into the culture of its members are the basis on which church planners have claimed that if you want your church to grow, then follow the principle of homogeneity. Seek those who share common attitudes and interests; form small groups where people can attach themselves; and provide programs and opportunities for involvement in order to ensure that everyone has a place where they feel connected. Most important in this regard is providing a Sunday school for children so that adults are free for worship and to meet other people. Where there are large numbers of like-minded people and these admonitions have been followed, the church has grown. This means the church grows in urban suburbs and larger, growing towns, but it declines and often closes its doors in small towns and in the inner cities.

Given the voluntary character of the church and the need to belong, the relationship of worship and the community is inverted. Instead of the community coming together to worship, individuals come to worship in order to form community. People "church shop," a phenomenon that is relatively recent. For most of history the community was a given; wherever the church was formed people already knew each other, worked together, played together, married, raised children, shared occasions of opportunity and success, and cared for each other in tragedy and grief. Worship then celebrated these events. Reflecting this integral relationship of the community to the church, the word "parish" originally designated a geographical area and not a congregation.

In contrast, as a voluntary community in a mobile society, the church gathers people who do not know each other. Cut off from extended families and neighborhoods of long standing, people come to church in search of community. Individuals may be adopted into small groups as if they were new members of a family. In larger churches, though, people must have enough in common so that personal relationships can easily develop. Similiarities attract. A young single person will find a sense of connection difficult in a large suburban, family parish where most of the energy is devoted to Sunday school for children, youth ministry, and events dominated by couples and families.

However, incorporating large numbers of new people because they have enough in common for personal relationships to develop also creates an insulated cycle. Congregations expend their energies on evangelistic efforts to attract new people; in turn, stewardship programs to raise money are needed to support further energies spent on pastoral and educational programs to assimilate and retain new members. This need is intensified by people's mobility today; in urban areas as much as twenty percent of a congregation leave each year, and the cycle of attraction and assimilation is never-ending.[2] No wonder the danger arises of focusing narrowly on the needs of members and the corresponding institutional needs of the church. And in this context, the danger is all too real that what is distinctive or normative for religious faith will be lost to the beliefs and attitudes of members.

Given the voluntary character of the church, the question has been raised, "Who speaks for the church?" More specifically, "How is the church to determine and sustain its identity?"[3] Unless this fundamental question is addressed, the church becomes unconsciously captive to whoever joins it. Still, what may begin as a "friendly takeover" may conclude in strife as different groups—in spite of what they share in common—find themselves at odds about what the church is and what it should do. Whether assimilation or strife, the crisis confronting the church is one of both vision and practice, a problem both theological and political: "What is Christian faith and, hence, that basis of identity in the church?" In turn, this question leads to another: "How must the church order its life in order to reflect and deepen this identity?"

The questions of identity and politics are central to addressing the nature and nurture of the ministry of the church. For example, given the institutional needs of attracting and keeping new members, the call to ministry often focuses on church work, so that lay ministry is then identified with the work of lay readers, chalice bearers, the altar guild, Sunday school teachers, and pastoral caregivers. This assumption is reflected in some of the exercises for gift identification which focus on the gifts for the upbuilding of the church and furthers the identification of ministry with work to be done in the church.

As a sales manager for a major company commented:

> In the almost thirty years of my professional career, my church has never once questioned that there be any type of accounting of my on-the-job ministry to others. My church has never once offered to improve those skills which could make me a better minister, nor has it ever asked if I needed any kind of support in what I am doing. There has never been an enquiry into the types of ethical decisions I must face, or

> whether I seek to communicate the faith to my co-workers. I have never been in a congregation where there was any type of public affirmation of a ministry in my career. In short, I must conclude that my church really does not have the least interest in whether or how I minister in my daily work.[4]

When this happens Christian faith becomes a separate realm divorced from the life and understandings of the everyday world in which we live. Alternatively, Christian faith unconsciously consecrates taken-for-granted views, roles, and relations in the world as God-given.

The voluntary character of the church makes easy the critique of the church as captive to the culture. Fair assessments, however, are difficult. While no doubt assimilated into the culture or creating its own distinctive culture, the church is always something more: a place of prayer and worship, a community of care and hospitality, a voice of prophetic vision and challenge. The transformative power of faith, many have claimed, is always possible given what has been called the "dangerous memory of Jesus" which we know and celebrate in word and sacrament—in the reading of Scripture and the bringing of that story to the present in preaching and in the reenactment of Jesus' passion, death, and resurrection in the eucharist.[5] In spite of preoccupations with what might be called issues of institutional maintenance, whether focusing on beautiful liturgies, stewardship programs, or the needs of newcomers, understandings of Christian faith and identity have also been significantly enlarged in the last fifteen years.

For example, baptism used to be a private affair of family and friends in which a child was baptized by the priest apart from the Sunday liturgy. Now the norm is baptism at the Sunday service. And as the baptismal liturgy makes clear, baptism is fundamentally a matter of initiation into the Christian community whose identity is more than a matter of belief.[6] After confessing the Apostles' Creed, candidates for baptism—or their parents and godparents—pledge, with God's help, to "continue in the apostles' teaching and fellowship, in the breaking of bread, and in the prayers"; to "resist evil and, whenever [they] fall into sin, repent and return to the Lord"; to "proclaim by word and example the Good News of God in Christ"; to "seek and serve Christ in all persons"; and to "strive for justice and peace among all people, and respect the dignity of every human being."[7] Reflecting the understanding of the baptismal liturgy, catechumenal processes have been developed which focus on initiation rather than instruction; these may be as long as or longer than a year in duration. In what has been called a post-Constantinian age of religious freedom and pluralism, becoming a Christian at least involves some degree of decision and commitment.[8]

However, these "signs of renewal" should not be overinterpreted. Catechumenal processes and a baptismal theology are by no means the singular or even common practice and understanding in the church. As a voluntary association, always having to attract and sustain members, members of the church may become nominal Christians. That is to say, in accommodating itself to those it wants to attract, the church may so fully mirror their cultural identities that new members become Christian in name only: nothing else is changed; there is nothing distinctive about their identities as Christian. Given these dynamics, the church must give ongoing attention to the articulation of the faith, ensure initiation and formation in the community of faith, and provide for critical assessment of the organization and structure of the church. Unless this is done the church will fall captive to the various attitudes and cultural assumptions of the people it seeks to address, serve, and transform.

The articulation of Christian faith may be approached in a variety of ways, but what Christians believe must be reflected in their way of life. In order not to sever vision and practice, I want to focus on ministry, beginning with the question of Christian faith and identity. In light of this identity, I want to articulate the task of the church in order to bear witness to this faith and to nurture the deepening of such faith in the lives of its people. An allegory may help to frame what is needed.

Once upon a time—not in the beginning but sometime after the beginning of time—there was a community that remembered its founder and sought to live a way of life that was like the one they had come to know. They shared meals together and gathered writings to tell the story of their founder. These they read regularly and discussed. This community was called a gathering, and they understood themselves as a distinct and different kind of people.

Some new gatherings formed quite naturally, like the birth of a household and the growth of a family. In time a range of communities were formed. Some people took jobs in the world; the community gathered once or twice a week. Other gatherings were more tightly woven together, and the people lived together. Some had gardens and sought a balanced life, including work in the gardens and time for study. Some gatherings formed schools and taught. Some opened hospitals, and some became community organizers. Varied, diverse, some simple, some complex—these gatherings still shared common features. They worshiped in similiar fashion, read from the same book, and spoke of common ideals.

Gatherings grew up on different sides of the mountains and across the waters. They kept in contact and on occasion came together. People would make new friends, sometimes shake their heads at how different things were, and worry about what would happen to their children. Returning home, they looked forward to coming together again.

A great city was finally built down from the mountains at the crossroads where river and ocean and overland routes met. Here peoples lived together, worked together, exchanged goods and services, and learned from each other. The city flourished, but in the city the gatherings often felt threatened by others, especially as different beliefs and ways were accepted by some members of their own communities. The city was not like a grand gathering together but often seemed more like a battleground of competing groups, each trying to attract and keep new members.

Like rebellious youth, different groups wore distinctive clothes, formed their own rituals, and expected initiates to undertake particular tasks. Feuds fueled differences. Often a group claimed that the story was not being told correctly. Others complained that the gatherings had become too ingrown. Still others, the politicians, sought a new structure and organization so that the gatherings would not spend all of their time in endless debate and bickering. As the nursery rhyme has said:

> Humpty Dumpty sat on a wall.
> Humpty Dumpty had a great fall.
> All the king's horses and all the king's men
> Couldn't put Humpty together again.

What we consider rise and fall—whether of an empire, a way of life, or of the one true, holy, catholic and apostolic church—is not a fall from the heights, but a sea change of rising and falling. As James Dunn, Roman Catholic biblical scholar, has noted, Scripture does not contain a pure faith, much less witness to a pristine church bearing an undivided witness. Rather, Scripture "canonizes...the diversity of Christianity." In fact, says Dunn, "perhaps the tragedy of early Catholicism was its failure to realize that the biggest heresy of all is the insistence that there is only one ecclesiastical obedience, only one orthodoxy."[9] However, if differences, conflict, and dissension have always been with us, the question remains and is perhaps even more perturbing: "What is the source and nature of Christian identity?" And more practically, the question is: "What is needed in order to nurture and sustain this identity?"

Christian identity as it has been given in the Anglican tradition is especially difficult to articulate because of the diverse movements seeking to renew or reform some part of the life of the church.[10] These may be described in a variety of ways. For example, Anglicanism may be viewed in terms of distinct strands of piety: one focusing on worship, another on spiritual discipline, another on social action, still another on evangelical renewal, and a final strand on reasoned reflection.

Movements of liturgical renewal are all but constant in Anglicanism, from Thomas Cranmer and the creation of the English Prayer Book in the sixteenth century to the nineteenth-century Oxford Anglo-Catholic movement to the contemporary liturgical renewal that gave rise to new Book of Common Prayer and the ongoing developments of liturgies for use in particular communities. Anglicanism is also marked by voices calling for "a life of holiness." Whether of Julian of Norwich, Jeremy Taylor, William Law, or contemporaries such as Tilden Edwards, Madeleine L'Engle, Carter Heyward, Alan Jones, Kenneth Leech, and the late Rachel Hosmer, these voices call us to a deeper relationship with God that challenges preoccupation with a narrow identification of Christian faith and the church.

The call to self-discipline in order to form a life of the spirit is challenged or complemented by other strands in

Anglicanism. Anglican evangelicals proclaimed justification by grace and the conversion of the heart, while others tied faith to a life of social action. Anglican evangelicals such as John Wesley, for example, placed emphasis on the grace of God and individual virtues; others, such as abolitionist William Wilberforce, tied faith to social action. Finally, when faith became hardened in dogmatic terms—whether in matters of worship, belief, or action—Anglicans such as Richard Hooker, Joseph Butler, F. D. Maurice, Kenneth Kirk, and William Temple offered reasoned accounts of faith in terms of contemporary understandings of the world. As the understandings of the world have changed, the understandings of faith have also been varied if not simply at odds.

Each strand of piety—ritual revivals, spiritual disciplines, evangelical renewal, social action, or reasoned reflection—seeks to express and deepen an understanding of Christian faith and the Christian life. These ranging voices indicate the difficulty in articulating what is central to Christian faith and identity. As each voice provides clarity and a greater sense of the demands of faith, the self-definition which each offers brings one part of the church into conflict with the larger church.

The ebb and flow of those seeking to deepen Christian faith and the Christian life through a variety of streams is difficult to contain within a larger river. Each stream goes its own way, and this "going one's own way" may be called the sectarian impulse. Identifying the church with particular beliefs and practices, a group within the church attempts to purge the church of differences, to purify or reform it, or, failing that, they form a separate community altogether.

This sectarian impulse is not simply negative; instead, it arises from our desire to deepen a religious way of life. In this sense, the sectarian impulse is part of the healthy pulse of the larger church and only becomes harsh, combative, and divisive when it is combined with the fear of being swept away by what we experience as a threat. When an abiding sense of common identity is gone, then the sectarian impulse yields to the sectarian politics that resemble those of holy war. Where this has happened, the sense of a common faith is gone.

Despite the fact that the eucharistic liturgies of the 1979 Book of Common Prayer reflect those of the early church, the liturgy of the church is not held in common. You can no longer go into any Episcopal church (or more broadly, any Anglican church in the world) and worship in the same way and feel an immediate identity in prayer. Similiarly, music has changed. Despite the canons, the hymnal has yielded to an increasing variety of hymnals and song books. Religious understandings may have always been different, but differences in understandings—for example, of scriptural authority, of God and providence, or of what is meant by death and resurrection—are increasingly striking. And these differences among members of the church become even more threatening in the discussion of moral issues, especially over deeply divisive public issues such as abortion and homosexuality. We can no longer assume a common identity in the church because we are daily confronted with a conflict in interpretations that is often confrontative, strident, and threatening.

The differences in the church threaten to tear us apart, individuals from congregations and congregations from the larger church. In another sense, however, our loss of a taken-for-granted identity and unity provides the opportunity to realize that we have sometimes been more English than Christian. Our identity was far more particular than we had realized and far less universal or catholic than we had claimed. In this sense, the crises that threaten to tear us apart are a call to conversion, to an enlargement of our faith.

Still, conversion and the deepening of faith are difficult because of the inability of the church to exercise effective authority. Quite literally, there *is* no authority—in the sense that there is no legitimate power to speak, to give testimony. No one has legitimate power to speak for anyone else, much less for the church as a whole. More specifically, the church has no authority that structures the teaching and discussion necessary for the establishment of identity, including (when necessary) judgments of what is true and what is false for Christians, of what is right and what is wrong. Instead of a structure that enables the teaching of the faith, the church has become fractured into distinct, separate gatherings or, alternatively, the capricious rule of the majority. And what is voted today may be reconsidered tomorrow or the next day when a new round of caucusing has been completed.

The failure of authority is most evident in the inability of the church to address conflict. For example, the church has done little more than call for respect of conscience in response to actions like the women's ordinations in Philadelphia in 1974, the refusal of some bishops after 1976 to acknowledge women as priests and allow them to exercise ministry in their dioceses, the refusal of some churches to use the 1979 Book of Common Prayer, or the ordination to the priesthood of people who are living in publically avowed, same-sex relationships. On moral issues as well—most notably on abortion, sexuality, and the justifiable use of force— bishops, General Conventions, priests, and theologians, among others, have taken and taught contradictory positions.

The apparent rationale at work in addressing conflict in the church has been that open discussion and exploration of different convictions is a matter of respect for individual conscience. If there is a broader rationale, it is that in the exchange of beliefs the understanding of faith will be enlarged and deepened so that, in the end, truth will win over error. However, the problem is that issues of conflict are defining moments for individuals and groups. Yet if there are no limits to the conflict, no point at which a resolution will be made by the church, the appeal to conscience ensures a never-ending crusade.

The crisis confronting the church is not a matter of the fall of the church; it is more a matter of the shattering of the church, of the breaking apart of the church. Warfare and disintegration arise not out of the struggles of conscience themselves, but from a failure of governance. The Episcopal Church, like other Protestant denominations, has failed to teach what it believes and to address and adjudicate the conflicts that divide it within.

In addressing issues of conflict the church needs to be clear when it is necessary to draw lines. By "drawing lines" I mean defining what is necessary for membership in the church, whether it is on matters of belief, liturgical worship, ecclesial polity, or moral convictions and actions. We need to be clear when we want to draw lines and when we don't. In seeking to claim our own faith we sometimes appear to draw lines when, in fact, we don't want either to include or exclude others. For example, Roman Catholics have acknowledged in their own tradition that Christians may be either pacifist in renouncing force as the way of Christian faith and witness or Christians may support the use of force to defend innocent life.[11] Both are viewed as faithful possibilities. Unlike the Anabaptists, the Roman Catholic Church has claimed that in this case no line should be drawn between pacifists and those who would use force in order to distinguish Christian from non-Christian.

In addition to questions about the use of force, other issues about which faithful Christians and Christian communities may disagree include whether the reserved sacrament (the consecrated bread and wine from the eucharist) should be kept and venerated, what eucharistic rite should be used, or whether charismatic gifts should be celebrated during the Sunday service. More difficult, Christians may also conclude that faithful persons may disagree about how God may be appropriately addressed (as male, female, both, or neither); whether abortion is morally justified, at least under certain conditions; or whether same-sex relations are acceptable and may be blessed. For some, however, conscience convinces them that Christian faith cannot tolerate a difference of judgment on these issues or other issues; for them, some resolution is necessary. For those whose conscience demands a resolution, the church's omni-tolerance deeply offends.

Teaching in itself is inadequate for addressing all conflicts of conscience. Teaching seeks to move toward consent, but that is what is precisely impossible on some issues. On those issues—however great or few they may be—in order to respect conscience the church must decide where it stands so that those who must may separate and form a different church. In fact, teaching and discipline work together so that people will be able to choose whether or not in conscience they need to form separate churches. Still, above all, protest and counter-protest, reformation and counter-reformation, the ebb and flow that create the deepening of faith in our lives is a never-ending process. The crisis confronting the church is not conflict in itself, but the failure to sustain the boundries of the community of faith in order to check the sectarian impulse and to enable the deepening of faith. As this suggests, there is no clear prescription of what to do. What is clear is that questions of identity and self-definition cannot be indefinitely postponed. To continue to defer conflict is not a matter of openmindedness but a failure to respect consciences that demand some resolution—even if it is resolved that we as a church will not have such an issue be a litmus test for faithfulness.

The sectarian impulse is not new. What is new is the increasingly democratic character of the church, which is fed by its voluntary character. As the church seeks to attract new members it tends to mirror their views and form its life in order to meet their perceived needs. Congregations develop something of their own character and attract people who are comfortable and support that character. A larger sense of the church is then threatened when these congregations differ and seek to realize their views in the church at large. The crisis of the church is first of all a crisis of identity.

Endnotes

1. For an historical account of the church as a voluntary association, see Sidney E. Mead, *The Lively Experiment: The Shaping of Christianity in America* (New York: Harper & Row, 1963), especially pp. 103-133. Also see James M. Gustafson, "The Voluntary Church: A Moral Appraisal," *The Church as Moral Decision-Maker* (Philadelphia: Pilgrim Press, 1970), pp. 109-137.

2. For example, this has been the case from the late 1980s through the early 1990s at St. Luke's Episcopal Church in Evanston, Illinois.

3. See Paul Ramsey, *Who Speaks for the Church? A Critique of the 1966 Geneva Conference on Church and Society* (Nashville, TN: Abingdon, 1967). For a recent addressing of this question in the Episcopal Church see Timothy F. Sedgwick and Philip Turner, eds., *The Crisis in Moral Teaching in the Episcopal Church* (Harrisburg, PA: Morehouse Publishing, 1992).

4. *Working Papers for the Lambeth Conference 1988* (prepared at the Saint Augustine's Seminar, Blackheath, London, England, July 29-August 7, 1987), para. 94, p. 27.

5. On the "dangerous memory of Jesus" see Johann Baptist Metz, *Faith in History and Society: Toward a Practical Fundamental Theology*, tr. David Smith (New York: Crossroad Publishing, 1980), pp. 88-94.

6. See, for example, Aidan Kavanagh, *The Shape of Baptism* (New York: Pueblo, 1978).

7. The Book of Common Prayer (New York: The Church Hymnal Corp., 1979), pp. 304-305. All subsequent references to the prayerbook will be contained in the text.

8. In the West, since Emperor Constantine declared Christianity the religion of the Roman Empire in 324 until the great democratic revolutions of the eighteenth century and the development of the modern state, all people were baptised as a matter of being subjects or citizens of a nation. This was called the Constantinian settlement. On the catechumenal processes in the Episcopal Church see, for example, Michael Merriman, ed., *The Baptismal Mystery and the Catechumenate* (New York: Church Hymnal, 1990); *The Catechumenal Process: Adult Initiation and Formation for Christian Life and Ministry* (New York: Church Hymnal, 1990); *The Catechumenate: Formation for Church Membership* (Alexandria, VA: Associated Parishes, 1991).

9. James D. G. Dunn, *Unity and Diversity in the New Testament* (Philadelphia: Westminster, 1977), pp. 376, 366.

10. The construal of the movements or "strands" of Anglicanism is often done in terms of high church, low church, and broad church or, in other words, in terms of catholic, evangelical, and liberal. This provides a focus on belief and "churchmanship." The suggestion of five strands of piety may broaden the sense of diversity and the basis of that diversity. For an historical overview of the diversity within Anglicanism see Perry Butler, "The History of Anglicanism from the Early Eighteenth Century to the Present," *The Study of Anglicanism*,

Stephen Sykes and John Booty, eds. (Minneapolis: Fortress, 1988), pp. 28-47.

11. See The National Conference of Catholic Bishops, *The Challenge of Peace* (Washington, D.C.: U.S. Catholic Conference, May 3, 1983), I, paras. 120, 121.

2

Discipleship and Sacramental Identity

D
ifferences and disagreements about what the church should do and teach, or what it should demand of its members, reflect differences both in understandings of Christian faith and the mission of the church. Those calling for a return to the traditional language of the older prayer book, for example, are in conflict with those who are developing new liturgies that seek to use feminine images of God. Conflicts over the ordination of women, the blessing of same-sex relationships, speaking in tongues, mission strategies for evangelism and renewal: these disagreements reflect essential differences in how Christian faith is understood and, in turn, how that faith is to be lived out. In this chapter, I seek to articulate Anglican understandings of Christian faith and the church in order to help identify competing claims and, in turn, anchor the church in an identity that is not merely captive to the culture.

In a course I teach on Anglican identity I begin by asking students the question, "What images or phrases do you associate with Anglicanism?" Responses vary but answers include Protestant and Reformed; comprehensive in outlook; diversity; grounded in Scripture, tradition, and reason; the Book of Common Prayer; liturgical and sacramental. These responses have remained fairly constant over time. My students clearly share a common sense of the church, but they are hard pressed to be clear about how these features reflect an understanding of Christian faith that Anglicans share in common.

The question of identity is not new to Anglicanism. At the time of the English Reformation in the sixteenth century, the Church of England was formed amid competing parties, especially Roman Catholics and Puritan reformers.[1] As a state church, the Church of England sought a middle way (*via media*) in which the nation would share a common faith. Central to this middle way was the rejection of particular views that sought to purify the church by defining the criteria for membership. Such particular views were held by both Catholics and Protestants. For Roman Catholics, the authority to resolve conflicts in understandings of faith and practice was divinely given to the Pope and exercised in the teaching and disciplinary apparatus of the church. For Protestants, this final authority rested in Scripture alone; in fact, this meant that authority lay with the ministers of the church, who had the final say in what Scripture meant. Both Roman Catholics and Protestants assumed what is called a positivist understanding of authority: the rule or law of the community was grounded on who said it; that is to say, its legitimacy rested on who posited what was said.

Anglicans, however, rejected positivist understandings of authority. For them, an understanding of faith and the demands of faith could only be grounded in an appeal to reason. Moreover, understandings evolve, and new reasons may be offered; agreement was not necessarily once and for all. Reasonable and faithful Christians could, therefore, disagree and still share a common faith. Tolerance and diversity of views have always been a mark of Anglicanism.

Sixteenth-century Anglican divine Richard Hooker gave voice to such a reasoned view of faith as distinct from Roman Catholic and Protestant understandings.[2] Specifically, Hooker claimed that the understanding of Christian faith was comparable to the process of understanding other aspects of human life. While conversion or justification—the making right of persons in relationship to God—is given in Scripture and through participation in the sacraments of the church, the understanding of that experience and reality is not given once and for all. Rather, understanding is historical. Through participation in the church and the world, our understanding develops over time. The past, which embodies the understanding of a people, may be deepened or even understood in different ways given further experience and new understandings.

For example, Christian faith makes claims about the source, basis, or ground of all life. As this is expressed in Genesis, God is understood as creator and interpreted cosmologically in terms of the creation of the world: "In the beginning God created the heavens and the earth...then [on the sixth day] God said, 'Let us make humankind in our image, according to our likeness'" (Gen. 1:1, 26). The meaning of this account and so the understanding of the nature of God as creator was, however, understood quite differently before and after the discoveries of geology and modern physics.[3] Before these discoveries of the natural world, it was quite conceivable that the world was only three or four thousand years old; afterward, it was irrational—against reason—to claim that the creation stories tell us the facts about the chronology of our physical beginnings. The meaning of God as creator has thereby changed and evolved.

So too for Hooker, Christian faith was not identified with a particular set of beliefs as interpreted once and for all. Rather, Christian faith was the order of life, a way of life, in which we participate. This way of life is revealed in Scripture. Our participation is made possible through the church and its sacraments. Beliefs are not of the essence of faith and should not unnecessarily divide the community of faith. Hooker, therefore, rejected the attempt to define the precise nature of the sacrament of eucharist or to decide in what sense bread and wine become the body and blood of Jesus Christ. What was important was participation in the sacraments and thereby the faith that was effected.[4] In this sense, Christian beliefs are a matter of interpreting this way of life in light of our broader experience and understanding of the world. Interpretation may vary, change, or evolve.

Our interpretations, therefore, should never be substituted for the reality of the faith in which we participate.

This view of Christian faith as a living thing may be helpfully grasped as reflecting the nature of understanding based on English common law reasoning, in contrast to Roman law.[5] For both English and Roman law, law expresses the order of things, how particular aspects of life realize broader ends and purposes. Roman law makes judgments on particulars by deduction. General laws are given; their application is a matter of deduction. In the common law tradition, however, there are no general laws. Statements about ends and purposes are, rather, generalizations drawn from the range of particular cases that have been decided. In this sense, the common law tradition that informed Hooker and is reflected in Anglican understandings of reason is historical, the practical wisdom of a people gained through their corporate experience over time.

In reflecting upon their tradition, Anglican thinkers have often claimed that the Anglican understanding of Christian faith is given in the witnesses of the apostolic age, specifically as contained in the Apostles' and Nicene creeds. What distinguishes Anglicanism from Roman Catholicism and Protestantism has, according to this account, been that Anglicans have remained open to new understandings: the meaning of Christian faith as given to the early church is not fixed at some later point in time, but is continually developing. In this sense, what is distinctive about Anglicanism and normative for Christian faith itself is the quality of comprehensiveness instead of some fixed content. H. R.

McAdoo gave the classic expression of this understanding of the integrity of Anglicanism, especially in his book, *The Spirit of Anglicanism*. The 1968 Lambeth Conference Report on Anglican identity expressed this same understanding:

> Comprehensiveness demands agreement on fundamentals, while tolerating disagreement on matters in which Christians may differ without feeling the necessity of breaking communion. In the mind of an Anglican, comprehensiveness is not compromise. Nor is it to bargain one truth for another. It is not a sophisticated word for syncretism. Rather it implies that the apprehension of truth is a growing thing: we only gradually succeed in "knowing the truth."
>
> It has been the tradition of Anglicanism to contain within one body both Protestant and Catholic elements. But there is a continuing search for the whole truth in which these elements will find complete reconciliation. Comprehensiveness implies a willingness to allow liberty of interpretation, with a certain slowness in arresting or restraining exploratory thinking.[6]

This vision of comprehensiveness has been articulated in terms of the authority of Scripture, tradition, and reason. Scripture and tradition—specifically the faith as given in the apostolic age—express the fundamentals of faith; reason is then the ongoing process of interpretation, of making sense out of the fundamentals. In contrast, the Roman Catholic Church has overdefined the faith by identifying what is fundamental with the teachings of the church and specifically the papacy. It may then claim that as an essential matter of faith, obedience to its proscriptions against contraception or abortion is required. No dissent can be tolerated. On the other hand, while Protestant denominations vary widely in their understanding of authority, their protest against the claims of Roman Catholicism have too often narrowed the understanding of faith to Scripture alone (*sola scriptura*). The way is thereby opened for fundamentalist interpretations of Christian faith and its demands that are even more positivistic than Roman Catholic teaching.

The understanding of Anglican identity that has been proposed by McAdoo and others may appear adequate, but it is not. The claim that there is some rule of faith (*regula fidei*) given in the apostolic church, some essential and unchanging beliefs, rests upon an ahistorical understanding of the fundamentals of faith. It depends upon an interpretation of the fundamental beliefs of Christian faith that is just as positivistic as that found in caricatures of the Roman Catholic and Protestant positions. In fact, however, individuals do not agree on what such a confession or creed means, nor on how to adjudicate differences in understanding.[7]

Just as the understanding of the meaning of God as creator has changed or evolved, so have the understandings of what it means to say that God is redeemer and that Jesus Christ has been raised from the dead. As with the creation accounts, the meaning of the resurrection has been tied to cosmology and claims about history, to what will happen to people upon their deaths and what will happen to the world itself. As reflected in the Roman Catholic requiem, the world will end in a day of wrath and judgment. In contrast, Brahms's *German Requiem* identifies the meaning of judgment with the knowledge that "all flesh is as the grass and all human goodness is as the blooming flower." Such differences in understanding are not derived from Scripture alone.

While resurrection is central to the Christian story, and therefore to Christian faith and identity, the meaning of "I believe in the resurrection" is not self-evident. Interpretation is required. Identity of faith is not given in some unchanging set of beliefs. What is necessary for establishing the identity of Christianity is an argument about the meaning of Christian faith in relationship to the beliefs and practices of the church as these began in the early church. This involves what Stephen Sykes has called a dialectical argument between the externality of faith as that is related to the inwardness of faith.[8]

Specifically, Sykes argues that Christian faith is historically mediated in terms of what may be called external forms, such as Scripture, creeds, catechetical and liturgical texts, hymns, sermons, writings, and the activity of worship itself. But such expressions of faith are meaningful only as they express the lived experience of the individual. In Christian thought, this lived experience is conceived in terms of conversion and reconciliation. The experience is one of grace and a new life marked by a new sense of power and freedom, trust, loss of self and love of others, openness to new possibilities, and altogether a new wholeness. This lived experience is termed by Sykes the inwardness of faith.

To focus on the externality of faith alone would be to be lost in the flood of particulars, in a seemingly never-ending range of texts, rites, and practices apart from what they mean to the individual. However, to focus on the inwardness of faith alone would be to be lost in abstract descriptions of feelings, attitudes, and dispositions. The inwardness of faith only arises in connection with the externality of faith. The externality of faith is only meaningful as it changes or transforms the human subject. Identity is not given by a singular, once-and-for-all understanding of the texts, rites, and practices that constitute the means by which Christian faith is mediated. An account of identity must instead develop the relationship between the forms by which Christian faith is expressed and mediated, and the changes that are brought about in the believer.

In this light, the source of Christian faith is the story of Jesus because, as Sykes claims, here is the conviction that "the power of God is at work in the creation of new life." As reflected in the gospels themselves, the story of Jesus Christ may be told and understood in different ways. There is, however, always the claim that in this story—in this person through his life, ministry, crucifixion, death, and resurrection—"the power of God to achieve something genuinely novel in the very midst of time" has been accomplished. Two convictions are assumed in this understanding of the source of Christian faith. First, to believe in the possibility of novelty and new life is to assume the basic goodness of creation, which is what Christians claim when they say, "God is Lord of creation." Such goodness, moreover, entails a second conviction. Not only is God Lord of creation but God is Lord over death. As Sykes writes, "If God is Lord over beginnings, he is Lord over ends. Already prefigured in Jesus' resurrection, it is said that God is Lord over death. Here the power is simply this, that human death is not the final word on his existence."[9]

At the heart of Christian identity, then, is the experience of conversion, of the change and transformation of our lives, tied to the conviction that something genuinely novel has been accomplished in the story of Jesus Christ. This claim is possible only because of the fundamental belief that, to use more philosophical language, the power of being is good. As phrased by H. Richard Niebuhr, "That which is, is good."[10] More specifically, creation is good, and death is not the denial of that goodness. In more theological language, these convictions are expressed by claiming that God is sovereign, creator and redeemer.

Continuing debate and disagreement about the meaning of the fundamental affirmations of Christian faith are inevitable. In fact, there can be no singular understanding of what these affirmations mean. Scripture and tradition provide points of view and witnesses of understandings from the past. New views arise as these sources are assessed in light of contemporary understandings of the world. In this sense the sources of Christian understanding are Scripture, tradition, and reason. In turn, comprehensiveness is grounded in this ongoing process of interpretation in contrast to prematurely ending the process of interpretation by fiat, whether grounded in a Protestant claim of *sola scriptura* or a Catholic one of papal authority and even infallibility. Not only is Christianity an historical religion in effecting novelty, conversion, transformation, and change in history, it is historical in that the meaning of these changes is only understood within history and therefore demands an ongoing process of interpretation.

When identity is understood in terms of beliefs, the question of identity is a matter of who is right, which views lie within the bounds of faith and which lie outside of the circle of faith. Disputed facts call for resolution because they threaten identity. There must be but one understanding of the meaning of God as creator or of the nature of resurrection. However, if beliefs arise from the attempt to understand, interpret, and make sense of the experience of transformation effected by the story of Jesus Christ, then identity is given in the story. The most fundamental question for identity is how to keep the story alive.

Certainly some understandings of the story of Jesus may place one outside of the community of faith. For example, to claim that the story of Christ gives believers a secret spiritual knowledge (some sort of *gnosis*) by which they can escape the evils of the body and the world is to deny the fundamental convictions central to the story. In contrast, however, it is within the confines of faith to argue about what is meant by good or what it means to be redeemed in light of human suffering and death. Scripture itself canonizes such discussion. For example, the writings of those who identify God's blessing with prosperity for the people of God stand next to the writings of Job, for whom suffering is a fact but not a punishment. In fact, such discussion and debate may contribute to making the story one's own, of entering more fully into the conversion at its heart. In this view dispute—far from being a threat to identity—is a sign of a faith that is alive. Instead of right belief, the central question for establishing identity is, "How is the story mediated?"

While the story of Jesus Christ may be known wherever it is read and heard, the story is known most fundamentally as it is enacted in worship. Hearing and participating in the story of Jesus, believers undergo a continuing conversion and transformation in their understanding of themselves and their relationship to the world. Theologically this is stated by saying that the church is present where the Word is preached and the sacraments are celebrated. In this sense, the source of Christian identity rests upon worship, not upon confessional agreements or doctrinal uniformity.

More specifically, worship mediates Christian faith as it celebrates the story of God in Jesus Christ. At the center of this story is the paschal mystery: Jesus reveals God—who God is, how God is present among us, what life in God is about—in his life, ministry, suffering, death, and resurrection. Here is the source of Christian identity, and here is the source that gives different forms of worship what Dom Gregory Dix calls a common shape. This story is the revelation of God. Worship is the source of Christian identity as it tells the story and helps believers participate in this story.[11] For this reason, baptism and the eucharist are the central, basic, foundational forms of worship. This was the case in the early church and in recent years has again been affirmed in the major ecumenical statement of our time, *Baptism, Eucharist, and Ministry*, written by the Faith and Order Commission of the World Council of Churches and also known as the Lima Document.[12]

Telling and enabling participation in the Christian story is what we mean by calling worship sacramental. As expressed in medieval theology, a sacrament is "that which effects by signifying."[13] Contemporary theologians speak of this in terms of symbolic realism: we are what we say and do. What we do and say forms who we are. For example, in marriage two people declare the reality of a covenant between them and thereby create that reality. In the broadest terms, then, Christian worship is sacramental in celebrating Jesus as the sacrament or sign of God to humanity. Jesus is the sacramental sign of our true identity, of who we are meant to be. In celebrating our identity as Christ-like, the church becomes the sacrament or sign of Christ to the world. Through the church's life, celebrated in worship, what was begun in Christ is continued in the life of the church.[14]

Among the most difficult problems in sustaining the church's Christic identity is countering its preoccupation with institutional maintenance, especially in those churches where membership is declining and budgets are reduced. As a result, expectations fall upon the clergy to make the church grow and to increase giving, so that growth in membership and increase in giving become the very meaning of evangelism and stewardship. Broader visions of ministry, and especially of lay ministry, stand as correctives to this narrowing of the identity and mission of the church, but visions cannot be expressed and realized apart from leadership in the church.

Paradoxically, in order to put forth a sacramental vision of the church in the world and to declericalize ministry, I want to focus next on ordained ministry and issues of teaching of governance. Before these more practical assessments, however, the character of Christian identity—of what we celebrate and effect in worship—may be extended by more specific reflections on ministry.

Too often new directions in "the development of ministry" are merely reactions to present practices. They capture a partial truth that has been lost, but because they are reactions, they fail to express a full and adequate understanding of ministry. For example, calls for fuller and richer lay ministry often rest upon critiques of the clericalization of ministry. Without an adequate theology of ministry, however, lay ministry is still identified with office and thus focuses on the range of roles laity may perform in the work of the church. In reaction to this, others see lay ministry in terms of service. Whether the focus is corporate or individual, ministry as service identifies Christian faith with service itself without making the connections between such work and Christian faith. The development of Christian ministry cannot be based on critique and reaction to what is perceived as wrong in present understandings and practices. The task and challenge for the development of ministry becomes clear only as the nature of Christian identity itself is clear.

The root meaning of the word "ministry" is service. A caution, however, is in order if we are to think through and offer a vision of what we are to be about as Christians. In the New Testament *diakonia*, "service," is not a specific role: it means rather the whole span of activities that build up the body of Christ, as in 1 Corinthians 12:5 or Ephesians 4:12. As Richard Norris has said, the basic category of Christian identity is not service but discipleship—to be followers of Jesus. Christians are called to learn, to share in the life of Christ, and to imitate. The New Testament is rich with these images. Jesus is the teacher; we are "children of God"; we are to be "in Christ." And always, we are beginners, called through practice to enter more deeply into the mind of Christ (1 Cor. 2:16).[15]

Given how abstract the word "ministry" is, a variety of uncritical understandings can come to define ministry very narrowly. In confusing ministry with an office or position, people ask, "Are you going into the ministry?" This identification of ministry with an office is reflected in Great Britain, where departments of state are referred to as the ministry of defense or the ministry of education. In this view ministry becomes something the clergy do rather than something one does simply as a

Christian, and so we say that ministry has become clericalized. Clergy as those authorized by the church assume the entire range of responsibilities in the community of faith: preaching, presiding at services of worship, evangelism, education, pastoral care, charity. When this happens, often unconsciously, a culture of dependence is created where people come to expect clergy to carry out the whole ministry of the church.

In reaction to clericalism, new emphasis has been placed on the ministry of the laity. This new emphasis can easily lead, however, to greater confusion in understanding Christian identity. Increasingly people speak of ministry in the workplace, or of ministry in the home, the community, and the world. Reflecting what has traditionally been known as individual calling or vocation, the focus moves away from the institutionalization of ministry in the church in order to focus on what individuals do as members of families and as members of larger communities—for example, as people with particular skills and training, or as citizens of a nation. This emphasis on ministry as something we do in our daily life and work corrects a narrow view of service as office; but, however needed and well intentioned, the word "ministry" still lacks any specific content. Whether the corporate calling of the church or individual callings in the world, when ministry focuses on the image of service alone, specific acts of service tend to become ends in themselves.

In other words, seeing ministry in terms of service rather than office has the advantage of moving beyond the notion of mere offices, but unless service and servanthood are connected with discipleship, ministry becomes identified with pastoral care, social services, and prophetic witness. The church's ministry is in this way narrowed to what has been traditionally called "corporate acts of mercy." The development of ministry is focused on the call to establish food pantries and soup kitchens, homeless shelters, housing coalitions, visitation and support of people in need, such as prisoners or persons with AIDS, tutoring—the list goes on. Ministry may be still be seen as a matter of the upbuilding of faith, but faith is identified with an ideal of human care and respect that is to be brought about through human action. The upbuilding of faith loses sight of proclamation and evangelism, teaching and formation, prayer and worship.

To live in Christ is to renounce all attempts to bring in the kingdom, to identify the rule of God with good works and social salvation. Rather, Jesus has announced God's rule, declared its presence among us, and called us to participate. We are, first of all, called to proclaim God's presence in our midst, to declare God's rule among us—in short, to evangelize, to proclaim Good News. Acts of love and compassion, faithfulness and fidelity, forgiveness and hospitality, mercy and justice arise as a response of faith, as a response arising from our recognition and experience that God is present. Only when this connection is made is the sense and acceptance of God's grace deepened in the individual.

Karl Rahner helpfully makes this connection between the acknowledgment of God's reign and specific acts of service when he describes faith as a matter of self-bestowal, of the offering or giving up of ourselves to God.[16] The story of Jesus Christ shocks us into acknowledging God's rule and how God is enfleshed in the world. This shock evokes our response of love and compassion. In the embrace and care of the Other, we are not seeking to solve a problem, but acknowledging and responding to God's presence in our midst. In the embrace of the Other we abandon ourselves; as we experience the presence of God, we are further disposed toward God.

If ministry, then, is the response of faith in the up-building of the community of faith, service that is faithful begins in and points back to the acknowledgment of God's rule known in and through the story of Jesus. The task of the church—the mission of the church and the ministry of its people—is to make this story known in the lives of its people. This casts a different light on the church's task. Christians are called individually and corporately to acts of care, hospitality, and mercy because these actions declare God's reign in the world and draw the world into that reign. They declare that the rule of God is not bound by the church but is always in the world.

The danger of ministry in the world arises when actions become identified as the means by which God's rule or purposes come about. "Servant ministry" or "lay ministry" are, therefore, misleading to the extent that they cause us to see Christian discipleship in terms of service as something distinct from evangelism. The work of service can never be separated from the broader demand of Christian discipleship to share the story of

Jesus Christ. While the category "ministry of the laity" may be here to stay, discipleship is a more fundamental and accurate description of the identity of Christians.

In the formation of Christian identity, the strength of sacramental traditions lies in their liturgical forms of worship. These ensure a certain shape to worship that gives the worshiper the space to pray what is said and done, to participate in the worship rather than to be edified. The danger is that liturgical worship can become a rote exercise in which worshipers are passive rather than active participants, where attention becomes focused on the style and beauty of the worship. Given the formal character of liturgical worship, the sermon is essential in making the connections and proclaiming the story of Christ as the story of our lives.

Worship as a matter of word and sacrament, however, is not in itself sufficient to form Christian identity. Worship celebrates and creates identity, but that identity requires more than participation in Sunday worship. This is especially the case given the pervasive power of contemporary culture with its ethic of self-fulfillment and its cultivation of the individual as autonomous. A Sunday eucharist may be a powerful celebration of Jesus' life, ministry, suffering, death, and resurrection, but however powerful it may be, worship in itself will be assimilated into broader cultural views unless explicit attention is given to formation. This is, of course, all the more the case given the voluntary character of the church. To bring new members into the church and sustain them, preaching and worship will tend to appeal to cultural values and understandings that are simply taken for granted.[17]

Christian faith, for example, is often couched in therapeutic terms: God "accepts" and "cares," enables us to acknowledge our wounds and to grieve, and brings us to wholeness. That God is also a God of justice and judgment is less likely to be heard. When God is seen in terms of history, God is all too likely to be understood to command and consecrate a way of life that looks suspiciously like the lives we lead—whether of middle class propriety (Jesus meek and mild), liberal reform, or prophetic renunciation. That God is the God of suffering and promises a victory different than our hoped-for social triumph—this is less likely to be heard.

Sunday worship alone cannot form a people so that God does not simply become our idol. Worship as the celebration of our identity requires the formation of that identity. Individuals must learn the story of faith for themselves, and this requires both reading Scripture and listening to those who seek to make sense of Scripture in our lives. For some, such study may be more academic than devotional. But whether it is Bible study, devotional reading (from Madeleine L'Engle and Henri Nouwen to *Forward Day By Day*), or academic study; whether it is work done with others, such as the four-year Education for Ministry program, or alone; whether education takes place through adult forums, workshops, or an individual reading program—some such study is necessary to learn the story of faith and make the connections in our lives.

The study of faith points to the equally important need to develop the disciplines that form our lives in the story of Christ. Christian faith is not given as a matter of knowledge apart from a way of life. Private prayer, contemplation and meditation, journaling, retreats away from the rush of daily activity, examination of life and confession of sins, friendships and fellowships, play and exercise, acts of hospitality and service: spiritual disciplines include all the ways in which what we do forms ourselves in relationship with God. In this sense, all people have spiritual disciplines. It is important for Christians to reflect on the ways their lives are formed and then form their lives in ways that will be distinctively Christian, but this need not be an esoteric exercise.

For example, I have convened conversations about formation by simply asking a small group or groups of people within a congregation to share with each other their disciplines and rituals. These disciplines and rituals are often taken for granted, but almost all people have them—rituals for eating, disciplines for reading and play, time for friends and for themselves, ways in which they are involved in the community with others. One question, with some time for reflection and discussion, is all that is needed. One such set of questions is, "What disciplines or rituals form your relations with friends, family, spouses? Are there disciplines and rituals in letter-writing, use of the telephone, activities together, sharing of meals? What works and what is frustrating?" The conversations confirm the value of choices and commitments that otherwise appear private and disconnected with the rest of life. They provide support in acknowledging common frustrations and concerns, limits and possibilities. And on the basis of everyday rituals and disciplines, people can talk about more explicitly Christian practices. How do people pray individually and with friends or family? How have they studied the Christian faith? How have they studied Scripture? What has been their experience in participating in a directed or undirected retreat? Do they meditate or journal?

Finally, formation of Christian identity, and more specifically the formation of disciples, requires a community that reflects the Christic identity which it celebrates in worship. For example, the community itself must welcome strangers, accept and forgive each other, and address the hopes, needs, and concerns of the world. Unless this is done, what is celebrated in worship is counterfeit. The story of Christ proclaimed and celebrated is held captive to the world, which is experienced as untrusting and unforgiving. What is said and done in worship increasingly lacks power.

These ideas do not indicate what precisely should be done in any of these areas of formation—teaching and study, disciplines of formation, pastoral care, and acts of love and justice. They all, though, are matters of discipleship, of living out and deepening Christian faith as a matter of response to God and upbuilding the community of faith. Ministry may refer more narrowly to acts of service and particularly to acts of love and justice. But if this is the case, the development of ministry can only happen by first developing disciples. Again, ministry is not in this sense the primary word to describe

Christian faith. If it becomes that, the source for Christian ministry is lost from view. This means, of course, that the task of the church is also lost from view, and calls for the development of ministry will be little more than rallying cries.

The development of Christian discipleship requires a comprehensive approach. One area of formation cannot be addressed in isolation from the rest of the Christian life. Just as the focus on ministry as service has distorted Christian identity, so too a narrowing attention to prayer and meditation or to forming the church as a community of acceptance and forgiveness will collapse Christian faith into a particular aspect of the Christian life. The development of ministry also requires that the leadership and resources of the church support formation.

For example, the resources of the church may be used in attempting to ensure that all clergy have the opportunity for full-time, paid positions. Such an emphasis is likely to come from clergy who have sacrificed personal resources in order to be educated and trained for a "professional role" and who then demand that the church fairly deploy those it trains. While such demands raise important questions, the time, attention, and resources of the church can easily focus on these demands—including how to support clergy in the midst of the present crisis—and fail to address other practical issues necessary to prevent the church from turning in upon itself.

In the remaining chapters of this book I want to address three issues which raise the question of the broader task or mission of the church and which, if addressed apart from the larger vision, lead to a fragmented church dominated by particular concerns and interests. First, I want to address the nature of ordained leadership and, in this light, the criteria for the selection of those to be ordained. Unless we come to understand and select ordained leadership in terms of the mission and ministry of the church, we will spend inordinate time and energy on supporting those who confuse their own needs and spiritual journeys with ordained ministry. Lacking any criteria beyond an individual's sense of calling, selection will be difficult, the need for pastoral support great, and attention to other aspects of Christian life limited.

Second, I want to address clergy ethics, not as a moral code but as the expression of the purposes of ministry. Here again, only in light of the mission of the church will the issues in ordained ministry be adequately identified so as not to focus narrowly on the interests and needs of individuals. Too often, for example, concerns about ordained ministry focus narrowly on pastoral relations and specifically on issues of sexual abuse. What are commonly called "boundary issues" must be addressed, but when they are addressed in isolation from the broader purposes and conflicts in ordained ministry, then ministry and Christian identity are too easily narrowed to interpersonal relations. The broader purposes and issues of ministry are lost from view. When they are not shared, the broader vision of discipleship and the support of the work of ministry—including the development of resources for such ministry—are limited or compromised.

Finally, the challenge in the formation of disciples is to be able to teach without falling prey to sectarian politics. Too often ecclesial politics works toward winning legislative decrees and administrative power in order to teach particular views. This then intensifies the struggle over control of the church in which new battle lines are drawn and forces mobilized. Such politics take on a life of their own. Given the voluntary character of the church, the problems of teaching, addressing conflict, and discipline are among the most difficult issues that the church confronts. I want then to conclude these practical studies of Christian identity with an assessment of what must be done in order to teach effectively.

Endnotes

1. For an historical view on this formative period see William P. Haugaard, "The History of Anglicanism from the Reformation to the Eighteenth Century," *The Study of Anglicanism*, Stephen Sykes and John Booty, eds. (Minneapolis: Fortress, 1988), pp. 3-28.

2. See John Booty, "Richard Hooker," *The Spirit of Anglicanism*, William Wolf, ed. (Wilton, CT: Morehouse-Barlow, 1979), pp. 1-45.

3. See John McPhee, *Basin and Range* (New York: Farrar, Straus, Giroux, 1981). On the relation of knowledge from the natural sciences to religious understanding see James M. Gustafson, *Ethics from a Theocentric Perspective*, Vol. 1 (Chicago: University of Chicago Press, 1981), pp. 251-279.

4. See Richard Hooker, *The Lawes of Ecclesiastical Politie* (Cambridge, MA: Harvard University Press, 1977-1981), V. 57.

5. For a discussion of Hooker's understanding of law see A. S. McGrade, "Introduction 1: Hooker's Polity and the Establishment of the English Church" in Richard Hooker, *Of the Laws of Ecclesiastical Polity, An Abridged Edition*, A. S. McGrade and Brian Vickers, eds. (London: Sidgwick & Jackson, 1975), pp. 16-20.

6. The Lambeth Conference (London, 1968), p. 140; quoted in Stephen Sykes, *The Integrity of Anglicanism* (New York: Seabury, 1978), pp. 9-10. See H. R. McAdoo, *The Spirit of Anglicanism* (New York: Charles Scribner's Sons, 1965).

7. See Sykes, *The Integrity of Anglicanism*, pp. 22-23.

8. Stephen Sykes, *The Identity of Christianity* (Philadelphia: Fortress, 1984), p. 233.

9. *Ibid.*, pp. 257-258.

10. H. Richard Niebuhr, *Radical Monotheism and Western Culture* (New York: Harper & Row, 1960), p. 32.

11. Dom Gregory Dix, *The Shape of the Liturgy* (London: Dacre, 1945), pp. 743-752. On such understandings as central to Anglicanism see Louis Weil, "The Gospel in Anglicanism," and W. Taylor Stevenson, "Lex Orandi—Lex Credendi," *The Study of Anglicanism*, pp. 51-76, 174-188.

12. *Baptism, Eucharist, and Ministry* (Geneva: World Council of Churches, 1982).

13. See Karl Rahner, "Introductory Observations on Thomas Aquinas' Theology of the Sacraments in General," *Theological Investigations* (London: Darton, Longman & Todd, 1976), 14:149-160. Also see "What Is a Sacrament?" in *Theological Investigations* 14:135-148.

14. See Edward Schillebeeckx, *Christ the Sacrament of the Encounter with God* (New York: Sheed and Ward, 1963), esp. pp. 47-82; Karl Rahner, *The Church and the Sacraments* (New York: Herder and Herder, 1963), pp. 11-19; also see Rahner, "The New Image of the Church," *Theological Investigations* 10 (London: Darton, Longman

& Todd, 1973), pp. 3-29, esp. 12-16, and "On the Theology of Worship," *Theological Investigations* 19 (London: Darton, Longman & Todd, 1983), p. 146; and Marie-Joseph le Guillou, "Church: Ecclesiology," *Sacramentum Mundi* I (New York: Herder and Herder, 1968), pp. 318-319, 323-327.

15. Richard Norris, "Notes on Church and 'Ministry' in Early Christianity," prepared for a consultation on a draft for "The House of Bishops' Pastoral Study on the Church and Its Ministry," March 18-20, 1987, Chicago, Illinois.

16. See Karl Rahner, *Love of Jesus, Love of Neighbor*, trans. Robert Barr (New York: Crossroad, 1983), pp. 69-71; *Foundations of Christian Faith*, trans. William V. Dyck (New York: Seabury, 1978), pp. 42-43, 76-80, 126-133.

17. See Timothy F. Sedgwick, *Sacramental Ethics: Paschal Identity and the Christian Life* (Philadelphia: Fortress, 1987), pp. 103-110.

3

Ordained Leadership for the Community of Faith

To ordain means to order, to arrange, to appoint. Ordained ministry, holy orders—specifically the offices of deacon, priest, and bishop—are "ordained" because the church assumes the responsibility of ordering its life for the sake of its identity and mission. Consequently how the church calls, selects, educates, deploys, and supports ordained ministry reflects and forms the identity and mission of the whole church, but too often what the church actually does belies any such vision.

One congregation I know in the Episcopal Church has five discernment committees, each with four or five members. Each committee talks with one member of the congregation who is considering ordained ministry. The committee is to help the man or woman "discern" whether or not they are called to holy orders, as well as to decide whether or not the vestry of the church is to recommend an individual to the diocese. The diocesan screening process is next, with the work of the Commission on Ministry. After gathering psychological tests, educational records, and written recommendations, the commission requires each would-be candidate to take part in a weekend meeting that combines the observation and assessment of individuals working in groups with a series of private interviews. Finally, the commission may interview those seeking holy orders. Recommendations for ordination from the Commission on Ministry must then be approved by the Standing Committee, the representative governing body of a diocese, and by the bishop.

The layers of review in the Episcopal Church are plentiful before an aspirant to holy orders is permitted to begin the education for ordained ministry. And each body—from the congregational discernment committee and vestry to the Commission on Ministry, Standing Committee, and bishop—has the power to stop the process at any point along the way. None of these, however, has the authority to make the decision that would actually commit the church to the individuals being considered for holy orders. This model of dispersed authority is little less than chaos; at the very least, those seeking to become clergy experience it as capricious despite the many well-intentioned people who are involved in the selection process. Moreover, because the dispersed authority makes it difficult to form and sustain a clear and shared sense of the purposes of ordained ministry, the sense of calling too easily becomes confused with individual piety.

Parish discernment committees, for example, may primarily discuss with individuals their journeys in faith and senses of calling, of what they should do with their lives. Because of this the ordination process provides one of the few opportunities to be taken seriously and to engage Christian faith seriously. Those seeking holy orders are, therefore, seen as religious, "holy" people who have a higher calling than others. In spite of efforts to renew the adult catechumenate in the Episcopal Church, the importance of baptism fades in comparison with ordination as a life-changing event, a new birth, and a matter of life vows binding a person to a new way of life in a new community. Moreover, this formation process takes place not in the local church, but in seminary, while in turn the church structures itself in order to support the new ministries of these people.

This vision of Christian faith and ministry is highly clerical, and it is also difficult to address because the church as a whole has such an unreflective and individualized understanding of the purposes and tasks of ordained ministry. Without adequate criteria, the basis for recommending someone for ordination is often reduced to his or her sense of personal calling, which is confirmed by a psychological understanding—or at least articulation—of their own inner dynamics. In introducing themselves to each other, persons seeking ordination will often express their sense of vocation simply by answering the question, "When did you receive the call?" A call, however, requires greater clarity about what someone is called to *do*. A job description is necessary if aspirants for holy orders are to have a sense of themselves as having the capacity both to exercise specific skills and the desire to do so. The vocation of ordained ministry is in this sense no different than other professions. While any given congregation or committee may share some common views, these do not necessarily coincide with those of the other groups making judgments in the selection process. The common basis for selection, unfortunately, too easily becomes sincerity of conviction and psychological health.

In order to develop adequate criteria for the selection of persons for ordained ministry, first of all the process of selection itself must be simplified. There needs to be a one-stage screening process. Individual congregations may initiate such discussions of vocation and calling. More helpful, however, would be diocesan conferences set up for the purposes of recruiting people who should seriously consider ordained ministry—instead of simply restricting themselves to those who present themselves for consideration.

The group responsible for decision-making, therefore, should be a diocesan group, either the Commission on Ministry or a selection committee formed by the commission. This would conserve human resources. Common understandings could be developed as these relate to the needs both of the church and of particular dioceses. Congregations would be able to support individuals, providing data where appropriate, without being forced to vote either for or against an individual. By the same token, men and women who seek ordination would not be caught in a series of recommendations in which they are passed on but never know whether or not they will receive final approval. With only one body making the decision, those seeking to prepare for ordained ministry are more likely to know they have the support of the church, or else they can "get on with their lives" and vocations as Christians in the world.

The development of criteria for selection, however, is impossible apart from agreement on the purposes and tasks of ordained ministry as a form of Christian leadership. The earliest forms of leadership in Christian history are the disciples and the apostles, those who follow Jesus and those who are sent into the world to bear witness to Christ. The graphic portraits of the disciples of Jesus in the gospels and the larger-than-life picture of Paul "the Apostle" became models for the Christian in general and for leadership in the Christian community in particular. As followers, the disciples were pupils of the rabbi. They sought to see what he did and to live with him so that they could come to represent him. The disciples gave up everything to dedicate themselves to Jesus.

Discipleship and apostleship are, of course, tied together when the disciples of Jesus receive the post-resurrection apostolic command: "Go therefore and make disciples of all nations, baptizing them in the name of the Father and of the Son and of the Holy Spirit, and teaching them to obey everything that I have commanded you" (Mt. 28:19-20). What distinguishes the apostles, therefore, is that they are called as missionaries, persons sent out to all nations.

The image at the heart of both discipleship and apostleship that has provided a model for all future understandings of the Christian life and leadership itself is servanthood—not simply as general service to others but as service to Jesus Christ (2 Cor. 4:5). More literally, discipleship and apostleship consist in being a slave to Jesus. Paul rejoices in this identification with the cross of Christ as it gives new life: "I have been crucified with Christ; and it is no longer I who live, but it is Christ who lives in me" (Gal. 2:19-20a).

For Paul, such servanthood is no abstract ideal; servanthood is doing what is necessary for the building of the community of faith, and doing all that he does in the name of Jesus Christ. For example, Paul appeals to the Corinthians to heed his call to them because he is seeking them out not for his benefit, but only because of the power of the gospel: "For if I do this of my own will, I have a reward; but if not of my own will, I am entrusted with a commission. What then is my reward? Just this: that in my proclamation I may make the gospel free of charge, so as not to make full use of my rights in the gospel" (1 Cor. 9:17-18). Similarly, Paul will appeal to congregations to raise money for the poverty of the Jerusalem church because such sharing is at the heart of Christian servanthood. At the center of his apostolic mission, however, was preaching the gospel. As reflected in his letters, this mission included exhortation, correction, and teaching.[1]

We have in this description of Paul's apostleship a description of the charismatic leader—literally, one whose leadership arises from the power of a divine gift—who is beginning to see the necessity for a more rational ordering of the Christian communities that he began. Charismatic leadership gave way to residential leaders who would preserve the newly formed communities of

53

faith. Suddenly, at the end of the first century and the beginning of the second, the reference to apostles fades; in its place we begin to hear of "elders" and "superintendents," which is to say, *presbyteroi* and *episkopoi*.[2] As reflected in the First Letter to Timothy, these elders and superintendents assumed responsibility over the material affairs of the congregation. They were administrators. While some labored in preaching and teaching, this was not their primary responsibility. Preaching and teaching still appear to remain within the province of charismatic leaders, those whom the church called prophets.

What is most striking about this description of the developing church through the second century is the lack of reference to sacramental ministry. Arguments from silence are always tentative and incomplete. It appears, though, that presiding over the worship of the community—from baptism of new members to leading the celebration of the eucharist—was not ordered. Leadership over worship was not restricted to persons specifically authorized by the community. For example, there are no references in Acts or in Paul's writings to a tradition of ordained presidency, and the *Didache* allows "prophets," as distinct from presbyters or bishops, to preside at the eucharist.[3] It is, in fact, not until the third century that bishops—and presbyters as sharing in the ministry of the bishop—are referred to explicitly as *hiereus* or *sacerdos*, as priests who lead worship. Authority to order the life of the community extended then from the management of material goods to pastoral care, teaching, discipline, and sacramental worship.

Richard Norris summarizes the development of ordained leadership in this way:

> What we call "priesthood," then, emerges in the course of the second century as an office of great complexity indeed....Their fundamental business is that of "shepherding," which is perhaps best translated as "ruling"; they are the supervisors of the entire life of the congregation....The monarchical bishop with presbyters is the authoritative teacher of the community, the trustee of the tradition which comes from "the apostles."
>
> ...This teaching office, moreover, is understood to be an aspect of ruling. The bishop and his colleagues are not in the business of merely suggesting or commending the truth they have received. Their duty is rather to guarantee that the truth of the Christian mystery, in its purity, shall be lived out and be lived up to by the people whom they shepherd. Consequently, their teaching office involves functions of admonition, rebuke, and judgment. It issues ultimately in "binding and loosing" (Mt. 16:19). Finally, their shepherding or ruling expresses itself in their presidency over the congregation's worship, which was in any case the focal setting of their official teaching activity.[4]

As Norris outlines above, the early Christian churches had to move from the charismatic leadership of persons such as Paul to a more rational and orderly form of governance by the community of faith—what Max Weber called the "routinization of charisma."[5] The experience of Jesus had to be translated into forms of worship, teaching, and a way of life that would express and pass on what was for the disciples and apostles the meaning of Jesus.

In order to ensure the integrity of its common life amidst differences and conflicts, the regularized appointment of leaders from within the community of faith was inevitable. It is another matter, however, for Christians to answer the question today, "What does this order of ministry mean for us, especially for our own understanding of holy orders?" The cleansing, if not perhaps sometimes caustic, effect of the history of holy orders is to disabuse us of acting as if the character of ordained ministry were ordained in heaven. Unfortunately such notions are not uncommon, often put forward by naïve understandings of apostolic succession that would have Jesus appointing sacramental priests after the Last Supper. In fact, however, the development of holy orders represents the ongoing effort of the church to organize and discipline its common life. That the church could have organized its life and ordered its ministry differently is surely plausible, but need not invalidate the order that did develop.

Until the third century, liturgical and sacramental leadership were not universally wedded to pastoral oversight and teaching, which is noteworthy for our understanding of the ordained office of priest. Yet this union of the sacramental with the pastoral became central to this holy order within the catholic tradition. Continuing this model, however, can only be justified by good reasons that can indicate how combining sacramental leadership and pastoral oversight serves the community of faith in deepening its identity and mission. These reasons may be stated in terms of four maxims, in whose light criteria for selection of priests may be developed.

First, Christian faith is an *ecclesial* faith. Conversion, reconciliation, and redemption are gifts bestowed upon entrance into the community of faith that is formed in the remembrance and reenactment of the life, death, and resurrection of Jesus Christ. This is most powerfully evidenced in the rite of baptism and celebrated in the eucharist.

Acknowledging their acceptance of Jesus Christ, trusting in his grace and love, candidates for baptism promise to follow and obey him through communion with the holy church. Communion itself is specified as continuing in the apostles' teaching and fellowship, in breaking of bread, in prayers, in repentance, through proclamation in word and deed, by service to others, and in laboring for justice and peace. What this means is that conversion and reconciliation are not a matter of something believed in but, rather, arise from a way of life. As Aidan Kavanagh has said, "The faith which results in concepts is first of all a way of living together— at peace with the whole of creation and its Creator in the revealed incarnate Word who is now become a people."[6]

Second, there is but *one priesthood*, that of Jesus Christ, which Christians enter by virtue of baptism into the community of faith. Christians are baptized into priesthood, not ordained to priesthood.

Third, sacramental priesthood is not one that offers sacrifices to God on behalf of a people; rather, sacramental priesthood can only be as a sign and sacrament of *the priesthood of the people of God*, which is effected in Jesus Christ. An order of priests to perform sacrifices and mediate between God and humanity was contrary to the gospel and the formation of the community of faith. As expressed in the Letter to the Hebrews, the idea of a new order of priests to mediate between God and humanity violates the once-and-for-all character of redemption in Jesus Christ: "He has appeared once for all at the end of the age to remove sin by the sacrifice of himself" (Heb. 9:26b). If Christians are to use priest-language at all, they can only say that Jesus Christ is the one true priest who through his full offering to God is one with God, as Son is to Father. We then are priests by adoption into the community of faith. In communion with the community of faith, we share in the body of Christ, in Christ's offering. In this offering of ourselves we too are reconciled with God. We celebrate the paschal character of this movement of faith in Christ in worship and in our lives, and as we enact this movement we deepen our sense of the presence of God in our lives.

It is now possible to propose why the ordained ministry we designate as priest should combine oversight over the community of faith and liturgical leadership. The person who has pastoral oversight in a community of faith—managing everyday affairs, teaching, and caring for individual members—is a person who intimately knows the members of the community, their sense of things, their hopes, their cares, and their joys. Members of the community cannot help but identify with this person who knows them and is able to give voice to their lives. Moreover, as he or she has oversight over the community, the priest is seen as representing the community and naturally leads it in worship—just as the grandparent who knows the life of the family most naturally leads the toast at the family gathering.

Leading eucharistic worship—saying the eucharistic prayer, breaking the bread, raising the cup—in turn enables pastoral oversight. As people identify with the priest's leading of worship, they become more open to sharing their needs, hopes, and concerns. Increasingly they are more open to pastoral oversight and teaching, including teaching that addresses the most significant issues that come before the community of faith. The reason for wedding in one office liturgical leadership and pastoral oversight is, quite simply, that they complement each other. The fourth maxim, then, is that *liturgical leadership and pastoral oversight* are ordered in the office of priesthood because they enable one another and each makes the other more effective.

As ordained, the priest is not only an individual Christian confessing his or her faith and living it within the community of faith. In sharing in the faith of others, the priest becomes identified with the faith of the community itself. In this sense, the priest becomes a *sign* of the community of faith, a sign of the common offering of their life to God as effected by Jesus Christ. As the priest shares in the life of the larger church under the direction of their bishop, the priest also comes to be a sign of the larger church and its catholicity. The priest signifies the people of God as a priestly people, a people who in the image of Jesus Christ offer and dedicate their lives to God. In becoming such a sign, pastoral oversight is further enhanced and corporate worship enabled. In this way, the priest is sacramental: the priest effects what he or she signifies.

The integral relationship I propose between pastoral oversight and liturgical leadership suggests why priests have been viewed as persons in touch with the holy, as bearers of the sacred, and as story-tellers. In *The Future Shape of Ministry*, for example, Terry Holmes held up the image of priest as shaman.[7] In exercising pastoral oversight and presiding over the worship life of the community, priests must be able to articulate the story of faith in terms of the story of the lives of the people. They must be story-tellers. In bringing together the Christian story with the story of our lives people are in touch with the holy. As celebrated in baptism and eucharist, the offering of ourselves to God brings about newness of life. But priests are not shamans, people endowed with higher spiritual powers, but participants in the story of Christ. They have different rather than greater powers than other members of the community. This power arises from the exercise of pastoral oversight and liturgical leadership. Their ministry is sacramental because they are signs for the community in our identification with Christ in the offering of ourselves to God.

A word of caution is needed. An ordained order of priests assuming responsibility for both oversight of the community of faith and liturgical worship is not without its dangers. Authority for teaching, witness, management, pastoral care, and liturgical worship can all too easily lead to the collapse of every ministerial function into those of the priest. The current emphasis on lay ministry and total ministry is itself a reaction to just such a clericalization of ministry.

This normative vision of the sacramental order of priesthood suggests criteria we can use for the selection of persons for that ordained office. These criteria arise from the relationship between pastoral oversight and liturgical leadership. They need to be developed in terms of these tasks, not in terms of spirituality as some separate power or gift or of calling as somehow separate from these tasks. At the most basic level, someone seeking holy orders must be a baptized Christian who is an active member of the church. More specific to ordained ministry, a priest must be able to speak and read aloud effectively in order to conduct public worship, and must have the leadership qualities necessary for pastoral oversight.

Pastoral oversight requires the ability to relate both intimately and broadly to members within a community of faith and, in turn, to articulate their perceptions, concerns, and hopes. Without this capacity to relate to a congregation and therefore represent them, leadership in liturgical worship becomes separated from pastoral oversight. Instead of representing the community in worship, the liturgical leader becomes a performer. Worship then becomes something that happens to the individual worshiper rather than something that worshipers do corporately in expressing and offering their lives to God.

This is not to imply a single standard or measure of pastoral oversight but rather to provide a more general principle. To insist on a single standard would be to establish a particular community as normative and to assume that what was needed to relate to members of that community was needed in every community. The distinctive identities of communities would be ignored. Different communities need different persons to exercise effective pastoral oversight.

In the same way, different kinds of people are needed to serve different congregations: rural congregations, inner-city congregations, highly educated congregations, or black, English, Hispanic, or Korean congregations. Different talents are needed in persons to serve effectively in missionary contexts where, instead of being called by a community, they must call a community into being. Still other qualities may be needed for effective priestly ministry as chaplains to the military, a college or university, a prison, or a hospital. There is no universal priesthood in the sense that any person can relate intimately and broadly to any congregation and, in turn, can articulate their perceptions, concerns, and hopes.

Criteria for the selection of deacons and bishops must similarly arise from how these offices of ministry serve the community of faith. The renewal of the diaconate has emphasized that deacons are to be signs of the servant ministry which stands at the heart of Christian faith. This servant ministry, however, is sometimes too narrowly reduced to the service of all persons who are in need; the deacon then becomes the church's agent for humanitarian aid. Instead, the deacon is to hold before the community of faith that the servanthood of Christ is always both proclamation and the welcome and care of those in need. In other words, deacons signify for the community that evangelism and service, in the narrow sense of the word, are inseparable.

Servanthood rather than service may better indicate what is central to the sacramental ministry of the deacon. Liturgically the deacon assumes responsibilities that would signify this servant identity for the community of faith. Reading the gospel, preaching, preparing the eucharistic table, and dismissing the congregation to "go in peace to love and serve the Lord"—these roles are assumed by the deacon as signs of what Christian service is about. The power of the liturgical acts of the deacon to form the identity of members of the community of faith, however, is minimal unless what is done liturgically reflects the actual role of the deacon in the community. In turn, where the deacon seeks such involvement in the community of faith, the liturgy may enable him or her to bring about the ministry of servanthood in the congregation.

While this understanding of servanthood is central to Christian faith, the early church had a narrower role for the deacon. Beyond particular acts of care and hospitality to those in need, the deacon served the community in a role more like that of administrator. It would be appropriate for the church to appoint some persons to fulfill this function. This again, though, should remind us that the ordained roles of ministry are not divinely ordained but rather the work of the church in ordering its life so as to sustain and deepen its Christian identity.

In the historical development of holy orders, bishops and deacons preceded the order of priests. The latter arose in order to act on behalf of bishops in presiding over communities of faith as bishops assumed oversight over more and more congregations. In this process priests came to signify and effect in their office and ministry the priestly identity of the community of faith as one of offering to God. Bishops in their office and ministry came, in turn, to signify and effect the unity and integrity of the Christian faith. We often speak of these in terms of catholicity and apostolicity, of a universal character of faith that we share in common and that is the same faith that the church has always celebrated and proclaimed.

In providing oversight, bishops are the chief pastors. This is not, however, primarily a matter of individual counsel and support. More accurately, bishops may be best understood as teachers: they have oversight over the development and nurture of the faith in the diocese and in the church at large. In assuming responsibility for teaching and formation, the bishop becomes the sign of the faith given to us through the apostles and shared by diverse peoples and congregations. The bishop, therefore, presides over liturgies when present and presides at the ordination of deacons and priests. Liturgically the bishop is a sign of faith that enables the church to hear and accept the bishop as first teacher and pastor. Task and liturgical role complement each other, each enabling the other.

The failure to articulate the sacramental nature of ordained ministry in terms of its purposes and tasks has not only prevented the development of criteria for selection, but broken the bond between bishop, priest, and deacon and the community of faith. Each order of ministry then no longer serves to build up the faith of the community. Instead, ordained ministry becomes a higher way until the resources of the church are narrowly focused on its clergy.

Endnotes

1. Raymond E. Brown, *Priest and Bishop: Biblical Reflections* (Paramus, NJ: Paulist, 1970), pp. 21-34, provides the basis for much of this description. See also Edward Schillebeeckx, *Ministry: Leadership in the Community of Jesus Christ*, tr. John Bowden (New York: Crossroad, 1981), esp. pp. 29-32. For the most comprehensive study on the development of ministerial roles see Bernard Cooke, *Ministry of Word and Sacraments: History and Theology* (Philadelphia: Fortress, 1976).

2. Richard A. Norris, Jr., "The Beginnings of Christian Priesthood," *Anglican Theological Review* 66 (1984), supplemental series 9:22.

3. William S. Adams, "The Eucharistic Assembly: Who Presides?" *Anglican Theological Review* 64 (1982), 3:317.

4. Norris, "Beginnings," p. 26.

5. See H. H. Gerth and C. Wright Mills, eds., *From Max Weber: Essays in Sociology* (New York: Oxford, 1946), pp. 245-264, 295-301. Ernest Troeltsch provides the classic account of this process in Christianity in terms of the formation of church and sect. See Troeltsch, *The Social Teaching of the Christian Churches*, 2 vols. (Louisville, KY:

Westminster/John Knox, 1992; 1st German ed. 1912), II:993-997, 1006-1010 for his concluding summary.

6. Aidan Kavanagh, "Christian Ministry and Ministries," *Anglican Theological Review* 66 (1984), supplemental series 9:42.

7. Urban T. Holmes, *The Future Shape of Ministry* (New York: Seabury, 1971), p. 246. This image is developed in his subsequent work. In describing the purpose of *Ministry and Imagination* (New York: Seabury, 1976) he says, "The fundamental issue in ministry today is the recovery of a sense of enchantment and the ability to be enchanting" (p. 8). See esp. pp. 219-242. In *Priest in Community* (New York: Seabury, 1978) see esp. "The Shamanistic Roots of Priesthood," pp. 68-95.

4

Outline for a
Clergy Ethic

An ethic has three tasks: to express the purposes that we are to honor and pursue, to make judgments about what should be done, and to direct us in a way of life so that we will see and do what is good and right. These tasks are undertaken when a way of life with its roles and practices has come under question. As ordained ministry undergoes assessment and revision, ethical reflection is expected. This kind of reflection is helpful when it articulates the purposes of ministry in terms of what has been and what needs to be done, but it also has its dangers. The danger of such reflection is that specific issues will so focus the attention of the church that the broader purposes of ministry are lost from view.

For example, the pressing need to address cases of clergy sexual abuse threatens to capture the limited resources of the church and, in turn, narrow the church's vision. The greatest concern in addressing instances of sexual misconduct is to protect those who seek pastoral care from the church; a sense of urgency comes from the threat of lawsuits against dioceses that will end by bankrupting them. "We have had several lawsuits brought against us for clergy sexual abuse," said one bishop. "We have to address the problem of clergy conduct." In response, several dioceses have begun to formulate codes of ethics and procedures for addressing the violations of these codes. They are attempting to take the side of the victim in investigating and addressing accusations and not to act as a shield for the clergy by preventing redress. Having clear public expectations for clergy conduct and a process for reporting misconduct, protecting confidentiality, providing counseling for those who have been abused, and disciplining clergy—all these are crucial for building trust that the church seeks the well being of its members.

Clergy conferences, diocesan committees, and bishops and their representatives are addressing the problem of sexual misconduct. Clergy define their pastoral roles, speak of the boundaries and boundary violations between clergy and those they serve, and identify what is needed to ensure "clergy wellness" so that their sense of self and the role is sustained and supported. As important as such work is, however, the broader purposes that ordained ministry serves in the mission of the church are too easily lost from view in the face of this urgency. Consequently, clergy ethics becomes a matter of negotiating policies and procedures for addressing sexual misconduct. While this is important, the development of a clergy ethic is so truncated as a result that other concerns and needs are silenced.

The crisis calling for the development of a clergy ethic is far larger than that of clergy sexual abuse. Discussions of ethics arise because what had been taken for granted is no longer so. To take an example from the field of medicine, traditionally the physician served the community; in turn, the community supported the physician. This interaction was conceived as a covenanted relationship between patient and physician. Physicians promised to care for the patient, to use their knowledge and skills to restore health, to relieve suffering, and above all to do no harm. In turn, patients placed themselves in the trust of the physician; their promise, as members of the community, was to support the physician. Yet all of this changed with specialization and the urbanization of medical practice. With advances in technology, physicians were no longer integrally related to a particular community; instead, they gathered in larger urban areas and served those with specific problems for which they had specialized knowledge and skill. No longer would a patient be treated by a general practitioner, but rather by an internist, orthopedist, cardiologist, obstetrician/gynecologist, surgeon, podiatrist, hemotologist, endocrinologist, or some other specialist instead.

With specialization, the personal relationships and mutually reinforcing expectations between physician and the community were broken. Patients became aware of how different patients were treated and began to ask what was to be gained from treatment. Such questioning made impossible the paternalism which previously governed medical care. No longer could physicians be viewed as wise and caring parents who knew best. In addition to questioning individual courses of treatment, moreover, the public began to ask whether or not health care delivery in general served the interests of the people. This questioning of medical practice forced physicians to address questions of ethics, both the ethics of particular cases and the broader purposes and principles that should govern their work.

What happened to physicians has also happened in other professions—most notably in law, in counseling, and in business, but also in technical fields such as engineering. In each field the development of an ethic is in response to the identity crisis within the profession, an identity crisis arising from the breakdown of shared expectations. In the church, the personal relationship between clergy and those they serve has taken longer to dissolve than in other professions. Expectations, in turn, have broken down more slowly, but they have broken down. The causes are many. Communities have become less homogeneous and conflicting expectations more open. Clergy are questioning their own roles and tasks in ministry, while for their part the church and its seminaries are asking what knowledge and skills are most needed in preparation for ordained ministry. Abuse of the ministerial relationship—no more vividly evidenced than in cases of sexual abuse—has been increasingly reported.

While the crisis of identity for clergy may be great, what little has been written about clergy ethics gives attention to only a limited number of moral issues.[1] To outline a clergy ethic in this broader context of Christian identity and mission may serve as a complement to these particular studies by identifying the range of problems that need to be addressed. Moreover, identifying the range of issues clergy need to consider will make concrete something more of what is the purpose of ministry and what discussions are needed in order to develop common expectations and understandings.

Clergy confront distinctive moral issues because of their role as clergy. While a "human ethic" or a "Christian ethic" applies to all people, a clergy ethic addresses the specific moral conflicts that arise in the exercise of the role of the ordained. Legitimated in ordination, clergy have knowledge and skills that others do not have but which others need or at least believe they need.[2]

Just as the physician has traditionally possessed the knowledge and skills for the cure of the body, the priest has had the knowledge and skills for the cure of souls. This gives the ordained power and authority over those they serve. For example, when people seek counsel they submit themselves to the wisdom of the clergyperson; in this sense, they are dependent upon the clergy. But even more than knowledge, individuals often seek counsel in times of crises and at major turning points in their lives, such as in preparing for marriage, in the grief of the death of a family member or friend, or in making a personal decision or commitment of faith. In these situations those whom clergy serve often seek emotional support as much if not more than practical

71

wisdom. They depend upon someone who cares about them and gives them a sense of meaning and possibilities. In turn, in order to be helped, they must be vulnerable, able to share their sorrows, anxieties, and hopes. When pastoral relationships work, those in need come to trust the clergyperson. The danger is that clergy may make a situation worse through offering poor or harmful advice, creating emotional dependence, or further isolating the person seeking care and counsel.

What is true in pastoral counseling is also true for other relationships in which clergy exercise knowledge and skills which others lack. For example, stewardship campaigns, strategic planning, evangelism, or teaching all provide opportunities for clergy to use their knowledge and skills for good, but also make possible manipulation and abuse. The professional nature of ministry does not, however, comprehend all that is connected to the experience of ordained ministry. To describe ordained ministry as "professional" says nothing about calling, about the faith all Christians share in common, about the nature of the sacramental character of ministry, or about how the relationships between clergy and laity are more than simply professional. What it does do, though, is highlight a significant fact: the power and authority that is given with the specialized knowledge and skills that others need bring their own potential conflicts and moral issues that are comparable to those confronted by other professionals such as doctors and teachers.

One difficulty in outlining these conflicts is the diverse training and responsibilities of ordained ministry.

In the Episcopal Church, clergy often have widely differing roles, education, and training. Specialities, for example, include parish ministry, pastoral counseling, chaplaincy, administration, public ministry, and teaching. A measure of the usefulness of a clergy ethic, therefore, will be to identify issues that all clergy confront despite their specific training and roles. In this light, common expectations and understandings of ordained ministry may also be addressed. Drawing from the framework of other professional ethics, the issues clergy confront may be described formally in terms of five areas: (1) obligations to self and others, (2) conflicts of conscience, (3) just distribution of services, (4) fairness in compensation, and (5) issues in pastoral relationships. We will consider each area in turn.

1. Obligations to self and others

Clergy identify with their office, with their role as ordained persons, because it gives them opportunities that few people have to share important events in the lives of others and to explore and profess what these events mean. Moreover, candidates for the priesthood increasingly enter seminary and are ordained in their forties, giving up the security of established lives because of their experience of the power of Christian faith in their own lives and the fulfillment of sharing in journeys of faith with others. The sense of "calling" to ordained ministry often arises from this context, so it is not surprising that for many people a "pastoral model" of ministry continues to dominate their sense of calling. Other relationships—such as those with family, friends, and other colleagues—do not always receive adequate attention.

Any clergy ethic, therefore, must enlarge upon this sense of pastoral responsibility and address the other responsibilities that individuals have to themselves and others. Questions about the use of time indicate the range of relationships involved: how much time, for example, should be spent in study, continuing education, diocesan work, pastoral calling, relaxation and exercise, family and friends, preparing for preaching, and work in the community? Critical assessment is needed on the relations and obligations of clergy to the communities in which they live, to the church, to fellow clergy, to families and friends, and to themselves.

One black priest serving an urban congregation noted, "For black clergy you can't speak of congregation *and* community. I was called here to serve the community." Most clergy, however, do not have such a clear sense of the relationship between obligations to church and to society. Whether through prophetic stance, silence, withdrawal, or social activism, clergy must adjudicate the demands of Christian faith and witness in the world with the responsibilities they have to the communities that have called and hired them. For example, they must decide what service they will give to the community, how much time should be spent in such service, and what social issues should be addressed in their preaching. They also must struggle with their responsibilities for calling the church to its ministry in the world and for allowing and supporting the community of faith in its own decisions.

The obligations of clergy to the communities in which they live, however, cannot be addressed and adjudicated without a clear sense of the other relationships and obligations that express the purposes of ordained ministry. Beyond obligations to the community, clergy have obligations to the church and to other clergy. As expressed in their ordination vows, priests in the Episcopal Church are to "share in the councils of the Church" and to "respect and be guided by the pastoral direction and leadership of [their] bishop" (BCP, 531-532). Moreover, clergy share responsibility for the work of the church that can best be done—or only be done—on a diocesan or national level. This includes, for example, the development of resources for congregations, including liturgical and educational materials; planning and support for creating new congregations or specialized ministries to persons in need; the formulation of church teachings; recruitment, selection, and deployment of clergy for the work of the church; strategic planning; ecumenical work; diocesan worship and other celebrations; the planning and design of the work of committees and other bodies of the church necessary to enable broad participation in the work of the church; communications; and all the other administrative work that is needed to make the work of the church go forward.

Clergy also have responsibilities to their profession to maintain their competence and that of their fellow clergy. Few professionals, except perhaps private therapists, work in such isolation from the work of their peers, in other words, without colleagues. Few professions, moreover, require such a high level of purposefulness. The work of ordained ministry—especially preaching, teaching, and pastoral care—is not about technical services but about professing and mediating a world of meaning, of making connections between the story of God in Jesus Christ and our own lives. This can only be done as the claims of Christian faith are meaningful to clergy.

Continuing education is one specific responsibility that clergy owe to their profession. Clergy need to continue their own study and reflection on the nature and meaning of faith. The focus on Scripture is needed but cannot be undertaken apart from reflection on the nature of God and the Christian life in light of the transformation effected in Jesus Christ. However, this is not narrowly a matter of individual study; the responsibility of clergy to proclaim their faith and enable others to make sense of faith requires conversation. Another person can affirm the integrity of our own development in understanding, challenge us, and enable us to communicate our faith in ways that respect and deepen the different understandings within the church. As well as the explicitly theological, continuing education for clergy is needed in a range of more practical areas, from management skills to knowledge about the whole network of social service available to people in need.

In addition to responsibilities for their professional competence, clergy have obligations to the profession itself. This includes ensuring educational opportunities and establishing standards that certify competence. As one medical professional who is married to a clergyperson commented, "It is ironic. We have programs and requirements for continuing education, but no money, whereas clergy have money but few programs and no requirements."

Finally, clergy have obligations to themselves, to their families, and to other personal relationships. Conflict in this area is never-ending when clergy over-identify with their vocations and take inadequate time for rest and leisure, for family and friends. Clergy burnout, marked by exhaustion and depression, is an all-too-frequent consequence. Attention to personal needs and relations is essential to what the Episcopal Diocese of Minnesota has called "clergy wellness."

Addressing the needs and obligations of clergy also requires coordinated discussions between clergy, congregations, and the larger church, for only in this way can common expectations be developed and procedures be instituted in order to realize them. For example, clergy search processes, evaluations, and contracts should express norms that reflect shared expectations regarding job descriptions, including responsibilities beyond the parish, regular evaluation, time off, salary and compensation, and continuing education. Dioceses need to develop these expectations through conversations with clergy, members of congregations, and diocesan staffs. In light of these conversations, policies need to be formed and communicated to clergy and congregations. Finally, ways of ensuring compliance with these policies have to be established; until they are, ordained ministry is reduced to a contract between the clergy and those they most directly serve.

Obligations to self and others is a broad area that, if fully detailed, would encompass all that is to be included in a clergy ethic. The other areas that outline professional ethics identify specific conflicts that need attention. They should also further illumine the purposes and tasks of ministry.

2. Conflicts of conscience

A second area in professional ethics in general is that of issues of conscience which arise from the conflict of obligations. One instance of such conflict for clergy is when they find themselves in disagreement with the teaching and discipline of the church at large. Conflicts, for example, have arisen for some clergy most poignantly in addressing the area of human sexuality. Sexual relationships apart from marriage, including homosexual relations, are affirmed by some clergy even though the church has traditionally judged such relationships to be immoral. Perhaps the most difficult have been the conflicts of conscience clergy experience with the larger church when they have decided for moral and pastoral reasons that they should bless a covenanted, same-sex relationship without the approval of (or in direct opposition to) the bishop. Here is an issue that may be formally described as a conflict of conscience between a clergyperson's understanding of what is needed and his or her obligation of obedience as a representative of the church.

To bless a covenanted, same-sex relation is in this case an act of ecclesial disobedience, analogous to an act of civil disobedience.[3] The moral conflict is not resolved by personal conviction, since here personal convictions have come into conflict with the vow of obedience to the teaching and discipline of the church, a vow necessary in order to sustain the integrity of the church. Disobedience is therefore either an act of schism or, alternatively, a public protest of the stance of the church.

As an act of schism, ecclesial disobedience is acting as if the particular congregation a clergyperson serves were a separate church or acting to create a separate church. If the intent is the public protest of the teaching and discipline of the church, then the clergyperson must act publicly and accept the church's judgment and discipline. Such a public act of ecclesial disobedience, though, involves everyone and may make impossible the pastoral intent of blessing the covenanted, same-sex relation. In either case, ecclesial disobedience would presumably be only a matter of last resort after, whenever possible, some accommodation or compromise is sought. For example, some Episcopal bishops have addressed the question of the blessing of vows at the pastoral level by leaving authority for decisions to the pastoral discretion of clergy.

Other conflicts of conscience that clergy may confront are those that arise between the promise of confidentiality and the need to prevent harm or do good.

These are most likely to arise in pastoral relationships or out of sacramental confession. Pastoral relationships depend upon a degree of confidentiality in order that the person seeking help can fully disclose their situation and needs. Someone confronting the possibility of divorce or someone with AIDS, for example, will be unlikely to seek counsel if they cannot trust that what they reveal will be held in confidence. In the sacrament of reconciliation the church and the priest as representative of the church have promised absolute confidentiality, what is referred to as the seal of confession. In this way God's forgiveness of sin is witnessed as unconditional.

The conflict of conscience arises most poignantly when someone is likely to do harm to themselves or to others. The suicidal man or woman, the man who has sexually abused children, the would-be murderer—such cases are rare but do arise. As with most moral conflicts, to do one thing is to deny some other good or obligation. What is important in developing a clergy ethic is to identify such conflicts and then to explore particular cases.

In this sense, a clergy ethic is not a matter of formulating a code of ethics, but of identifying and exploring issues in order to build common expectations that indicate what clergy should do and why they ought to do it. In this way the creation of shared expectations will sustain the identity of the ordained in terms of their service to the church in its mission.

3. Just distribution of services

A third area essential to a clergy ethic is that of the just distribution of services, the ordering of the range of obligations of clergy and the church. These obligations include those owed to all people in need, to the community in which a clergyperson lives, to the congregation that pays the clergyperson's salary, and to the diocese and its ministry. For example, how should the needs in the community—whether outreach ministry or pastoral counseling of those in chronic crisis—be balanced with specific responsibilities to the congregation such as preaching, teaching, and administration? Which responsibilities have priority?

The question of the just distribution of services is not narrowly a matter confronting individual clergy. More important are institutional questions regarding how clergy are recruited, trained, deployed, and supported in their ministries. And beyond the focus on ordained ministry, the church needs to address the other resources and services it develops, supports, and distributes. Such resources range from liturgical and teaching materials to direct financial grants that support congregations, specialized ministries to those in need, and individuals and groups.

The universalism of Christian mission has envisioned service to all people, a church that reached to the ends of the earth and that embraced all peoples, rich and poor, healthy and sick, young and old. However, the resources of the church have always been limited. Implicit or explicit strategies for the deployment of limited resources have always been adopted; strategies are inevitable. What is important is that these decisions be made carefully and deliberately, so that what is done reflects deeper convictions. The allocation of resources for small churches, whether rural or urban, is a good example that illustrates the questions of distributive justice that need to be addressed. Similiar questions need to be raised in addressing specialized ministries such chaplaincies, institutional support for evangelism and the beginning of new congregations, or the support of direct social ministries such as shelters for the homeless and food pantries.

Increasingly, neither small churches nor the church at large are either able or willing to support full-time, ordained ministry for the small church. In response, strategies for maintaining these churches often turn to raising up non-stipendiary, indigenous lay leadership from within the congregation. These leaders are then educated and trained in order to provide knowledge and skills that are viewed as important to the community of faith, such as administration or providing pastoral outreach. Others are ordained as priests with responsibilities for leading the community in its eucharistic worship. Sometimes these programs appear to be survival strategies; at other times they reflect well-thought-out theological convictions. The outstanding question in allocating resources for small churches, however, is whether or not the development and distribution of resources is fair.

Dioceses and larger churches can too easily see the development of indigenous ministry as adequate for addressing the needs of small churches, given their limited resources. Implicit in such a judgment is their belief that each church should be self-sufficient and that resources should be distributed on the basis of the ability to pay. As a consequence, education, training, deployment, and the resources of the church in general are focused on larger churches that can afford to pay for them. If the mission of the church goes beyond individual congregations, however, questions of recruitment, training, deployment, and support must be assessed and addressed more critically.

Questions of the distribution of resources to sustain the presence of the church in serving small communities may be further complicated by previous obligations and commitments. For example, denominational missionaries evangelized Native American peoples, and these peoples are now formed both by Christianity and by Native American traditions. They are blessed or caught—depending upon the perspective—between two cultures. Having evangelized the Native American peoples in the first place, the church now has an obligation to support Native American congregations and ensure adequate resources to enable them to form and deepen their identities as Native American Christians. In turn, other obligations may limit or even override the obligations to these congregations. Initiating new missions to new communities at the expense of Native American communities would appear unjust. However, the question of continuing financial support of the office of the bishop in order to provide leadership for the entire diocese, Native American congregations included, is a more complex conflict to resolve. The task of an ethic is not to answer these questions but rather to provide a framework for identifying such issues in order to enable decision-making.

4. Fairness in compensation

Integral to the problems of the distribution of services is a fourth set of issues, those of compensation. The question simply stated is, "Who pays for what services?" As I suggested previously in addressing obligations to self and others, clarity is needed in contracting between clergy and those who hire them. This requires more than a contract for the purchase of services by a congregation or some other organization. As clergy exercise ordained ministries—literally, ministries ordered by the church for the sake of the church—compensation must be sufficient in order to enable clergy to meet these obligations, including those to the community beyond their cures, to the larger church, to other clergy, and to their own professional development. Broad discussions of the purposes and tasks of ministry are needed in order to achieve the shared understandings for what clergy are being compensated. Again, this cannot be done by individual clergy and congregations but must also include denominational judicatories.

Compensation itself may be based on criteria of merit, such as past experience, education and training, and personal qualities. The problem with basing compensation on merit is the difficulty of reaching agreement on criteria, deciding who should make judgments, and applying criteria in making judgments. For example, the judgment of who is the best preacher or most able to provide pastoral care will vary among congregations. To base compensation on such judgments of merit made by congregations is to further a congregational view of the church and ordained ministry—especially if compensation is also a matter of the ability or willingness of the congregation to pay.

In contrast, a diocesan compensation committee may develop a compensation schedule based on criteria of merit. The difficulty in developing and applying common criteria, however, can result in compensation based simply on the longevity of service. In contrast to compensation based on merit, it may be argued that compensation should be equalized on the basis that "equals should be treated equally." In this case, despite differences in jobs and qualifications, the work of clergy is fundamentally equal in bearing witness to Christian faith and should not be distinguished by differences in compensation. Finally, compensation may be based on need. All compensation should at least meet certain basic needs; it is on this basis that the church provides disability payments to those who need them and distributes the cost to all.

In addition to clergy salaries, questions of fairness in compensation must be raised about retirement benefits. In the Episcopal Church these benefits are based on the salaries paid by individual congregations. This suggests that compensation is based either on the ability of a congregation to pay or else on individual merit, in which case it follows that the larger, more prosperous congregations require more expertise and attract better clergy.

As is often the case in developing public or ecclesial policies, ideal principles must be weighed against practical considerations, including what criteria may be reasonably agreed upon and fairly applied. This has meant that for most denominations compensation has aspects that reflect all three criteria—merit, need, and an egalitarian principle of basic equality. These are, however, too often not stated. When an overall rationale is missing, debate is inhibited, consensus is lost, and the potential for divisiveness is increased.

Conflicts of interest around the use of money also need attention, including specific issues like the use of honoraria, discretionary funds, and accounting for the use of monies. Should, for example, clergy receive compensation for special services such as weddings, funerals, and counseling? If they do, when and on what basis should they receive compensation, and then what should be done with the money received? Should it be income for the church or a supplement to clergy income for personal use? The underlying question is the relationship of work and pay, especially if the work of clergy as ordained ministers of the church includes service beyond the immediate cure and for which the cure is compensating. However, some work of clergy is the result of training and experience that is independent of ordained ministry or is undertaken above and beyond the assumed responsibilities and obligations. This work, it may be argued, is fairly compensated as work that falls outside of and in addition to the responsibilities of an ordained person.

Here, as elsewhere, there are significant disparities in the practices of clergy. Again, the importance of a clergy ethic is not to resolve these differences in terms of principles, but to identify those areas where further discussion is needed and to provide some principles for action as a framework for these discussions. The purposes of ministry and norms of action may be articulated, but these will not be moral fiats so much as the reasoned accounts of understandings and expectations. An ethic of norms and principles, in this sense, is effective in forming the practice of ordained ministry only as it arises from and returns to the discussion of cases.

5. Issues in pastoral relationships

What may be called pastoral or ministerial relations is a final area for moral reflection that may specify further the obligations of clergy to the persons they serve. The word "pastoral" itself points to the source of a number of obligations. Whether in areas like teaching, counseling, or spiritual direction, or in more general activities such as preaching and evangelization, clergy provide guidance for others. As reflected in the literature on professional ethics, four moral issues stand out. These may be designated in terms of competence, respect for autonomy, conflict of interest, and confidentiality.[4]

As reflected above in obligations to the profession, ministerial relationships depend upon the professional

competence of clergy. Ordination assumes certain qualifications. For example, the canons of the church require
that clergy be examined in Scripture, church history,
theology, ethics, contemporary society, liturgics, and
"the theory and practice of ministry."[5] These are necessary competencies if clergy are to enable others to make
sense of their own lives in terms of the meaning of
Christian faith. Apart from such knowledge, the church
lacks an essential warrant for ordination.

Not only must clergy be competent, but those they
serve must believe that they are competent. A pastoral
relationship depends upon a basic trust that clergy can
provide guidance in certain matters. The church and the
clergy are, therefore, responsible for recruiting and se-
lecting able candidates for ordination and for ensuring
the adequacy of their education and training. In turn,
individual clergy must engage those whom they serve or
who seek their services with candor in order to ensure
honest communication about their competence. This requires clarity about what they are and are not seeking to
accomplish.

Communicating competence is itself a part of the obligation of clergy to respect what philosophers have
called the autonomy of persons. What this phrase con-
veys is that to be a person is to have the power of self-
determination. To be human is not to be coerced, but
to will or consent to an action. The difficulty is that the
person seeking direction or guidance is in need and,
therefore, may accept what is said or suggested without
deliberate consent. Clergy, like other professionals, have
then a responsibility to indicate alternative under-

standings and other possible courses of action so that the people they work with can make free and knowledgeable decisions.

The third issue in ministerial relations is determining what limitations or restrictions should be placed on the relationships of clergy with those they serve. This is spoken of most frequently in terms of the "boundaries" in ministerial relations. Boundaries indicate specific conditions that are necessary for the ministerial relationship. To take an example from another profession, physicians do not treat their own children because a child's ability to express feelings and to make choices may be compromised by the desire to please or obey the wishes of the parent. In turn, the mother or father physician may be unable to make a competent decision regarding possible treatments because of her or his involvement with the child and desire for a specific outcome. Clergy are similarly limited. Whether at times of making life commitments—as in marriage or vocation—or in times of grief, clergy may support members of their family and close personal friends, but they will not be able to offer the pastoral guidance that they are able to offer to others. Understanding the limits of their competence and having respect for the autonomy of those close to them, clergy must set limits that define their ministerial relation.

Some relations are clearly incompatible with a pastoral relationship, such as when a pastoral relationship changes into a sexual relationship.[6] Whether providing spiritual direction or care and support at a time of crisis, pastoral relations are often marked by intimacy and the need for acceptance and affirmation. Clergy are often idealized as wise caregivers, and for this reason women have been especially vulnerable to the sexual advances of male clergy. The relationship, however, was not begun on equal terms but arose in the context of dependency and idealization. The change in relationship from pastoral to sexual is a change in roles; the boundaries of the relationship have been changed. As this violates the expectations and trust of those seeking pastoral care, such actions are called "boundary violations." Not only do they harm individuals, they also undermine a broader trust in the clergy as those able to provide pastoral care.

While the nature of boundary violations may appear clear, the relationships of clergy to members of their congregations are not always so clear. A clergy ethic provides a framework for the discussion of cases in order to develop a consensus about what should be done. For example, is it necessary for clergy only to date persons outside of the congregations or other cures they serve? Or, once a relationship between a clergyperson and a parishioner begins, does this mean that they cannot share in the life and worship of the same community of faith? Such questions point to the kind of discussion that is needed.

Confidentiality provides a final focus in assessing the distinctive moral issues raised by the ministerial relationship. As in the relationship between therapist and patient, confidentiality in the ministerial relationship is established in order to enable and strengthen the pastoral relationship. As discussed above in terms of conflicts of conscience, historically confidentiality has been at the very heart of the relation between priest and penitent. Priests have held in confidence the content of confessions in order to enable confession and to witness that God's forgiveness and grace is unconditional. The seal of confession has been understood as inviolable. Moral discussions are needed to clarify when a confession is sealed in confidentiality and how to communicate these boundaries.

Beyond sacramental confession, confidentiality is necessary in all pastoral relationships. As the pastoral relationship is to care for the other, knowledge from this relationship cannot be used in ways that would harm the person. Again, breaking confidences undermines the trust necessary for enabling pastoral relations. The moral question, however, arises in cases when holding knowledge in confidence may do harm to the person who has confided in the clergyperson or may do harm to others. Two questions identify the most troubling cases. First, should confidences be broken either to prevent harm or to benefit the person who has confided thoughts of suicide to a clergyperson? Second, should confidentiality give way to the needs of others, as when child abuse is revealed in a pastoral relationship? In light of the discussion of particular cases, the boundaries of confidentiality may begin to be understood. Equally important is how well these boundaries are communicated to those who are in the care of clergy.

The purpose of a clergy ethic is not to set out a code of behavior. Codes are formed only after there is consensus about what ought to be done. A clergy ethic is first of all a framework in which to discuss particular cases in light of the moral issues that arise for clergy as people who have specific roles to play and specialized knowledge and skills. Some framework is necessary or cases will either be too narrowly focused or so varied that critical reflection is impossible. Focusing on conflicting duties, issues of conscience, the distribution of services, questions of compensation, and the nature of the pastoral relationship is one way to frame these moral issues. Other frameworks may be developed in light of cases, but what is important are the conversations that illumine particular cases. Principles and rules that should govern behavior may be formulated, but only as they arise from cases will principles and rules be statements of consensus about the purposes of ordained ministry and how these purposes are to be realized.

What may be most helpful in developing a clergy ethic is the development and discussion of cases in groups of clergy and laity. Cases could then be collected and collated for further discussion; that is how other codes of professional ethics have developed. And while from this process statements of principles and rules have been formulated, what has been most important is the process itself. The discussions hold the promise of sharing the vision and sense of vocation that persons have for ordained ministry and the church and its mission as well.

Endnotes

1. See, for example, Karen Lebacqz, *Professional Ethics: Power and Paradox* (Nashville: Abingdon, 1985); Gaylord Noyce, *Pastoral Ethics: Professional Responsibilities of Clergy* (Nashville: Abingdon, 1988); and Walter E. Wiest and Elwyn A. Smith, *Ethics in Ministry: A Guide for the Professional* (Minneapolis: Fortress, 1990). On the overall nature of ethics see James M. Gustafson, *Protestant and Roman Catholic Ethics* (Chicago: University of Chicago Press, 1978), esp. pp. 138-144.

2. The construing of the distinctive moral issues is informed by the issues confronted by professional ethics. See Michael D. Bayles, *Professional Ethics* (Belmont, CA: Wadsworth, 2nd ed., 1989). On the ways in which clergy are and are not professionals see Paul F. Camenisch, "Clergy Ethics and the Professional Ethics Model," *Clergy Ethics in a Changing Society*, James P. Wind, Russell Burck, Paul Camenisch, and Dennis McCann, eds. (Louisville, KY: Westminster/John Knox, 1991), pp. 114-133.

3. The issues involving ecclesial disobedience may be helpfully compared with those of civil disobedience. On civil disobedience see James Childress, *Civil Disobedience and Political Obligations* (New Haven, CT: Yale University Press, 1971).

4. For a study of the ethical issues of confidentiality, informed consent, and evangelism or what she calls "convert seeking," see Margaret P. Battin, *Ethics in the Sanctuary: Examining the Practices of Organized Religion* (New Haven, CT: Yale University Press, 1990).

5. See *Constitution & Canons* (revised 1991), Title III, canon 6, section 4.

6. See Marie M. Fortune, *Is Nothing Sacred?: When Sex Invades the Pastoral Relationship* (San Francisco: Harper & Row, 1989), and Ronald G. Barton and Karen Lebacqz, *Sex in the Parish* (Louisville, KY: Westminster/John Knox, 1991).

5

The Politics of Piety

Whether they are addressing questions of Christian identity, deciding which people should be ordained, or developing a clergy ethic, people and groups tend to substitute their own points of view for the more comprehensive Anglican understanding of Christian faith. This tendency may be called the problem of idolatry and, as such, it is part of the human condition. Idolatry, though, is exacerbated by the voluntary character of the church. As I said in the first chapter, because people join the church of their own free will, they have a high level of commitment; however, since the church still has the task of attracting and retaining its members, the attitudes and views of parishioners tend to reflect the dominant culture in which they live. Comprehensiveness and breadth of viewpoint is, therefore, often lacking in individual congregations; different congregations reflect different communities and cultures in the society. Here is the opportunity both for catholicity and for incendiary warfare.

Without a unifying vision of Christian faith that is reflected in the way the church does its business, partisan groups seek to resolve differences by legislative fiat. Whether the issue is one of liturgical change, the ordination of women, abortion, homosexual relations, or the use of military force, an increasing number of Episcopalians approach these questions from a legislative mentality.

As Robert Wuthnow describes in *The Struggle for America's Soul*,[1] the divisive politics in the Episcopal Church reflect changes in what may be called the religious right and the secular and religious left. Before the 1960s, conservative evangelicals of the religious right were largely marginal to the broader society. Bible churches, pentecostals, and holiness sects were concerned with their own communities and particularly with the family as the basic unit of church and society. The conservative evangelicals of Lynchburg, Virginia, or Tulsa, Oklahoma, were worlds unto themselves, far apart from state capitals or from Washington, D.C.

With the sixties, all that changed. The sexual revolution, women's liberation, abortion, gay and lesbian rights, alternative life styles—all these threatened the religious right. While individual members of the right reacted differently to different issues, each one was seen as part of a broader attack on the family, the church, and society itself. The sexual revolution and its demands for liberation could only be conceived as rebellion against God. Political action in the local community as well as action directed toward state and national government became urgent, and so the ongoing politicization of the religious right began. To be a conservative evangelical today is to be pro-family and to work politically to restore America as "one nation under God."

On the opposite end of the political spectrum are the unchurched, the secular humanists, and some members of the religious left such as Unitarians and secular Jews. The values and ideals of the secular and religious left are those of the city, including pluralism, acceptance, and toleration of others. Many of these people have themselves escaped from the confines of more rural America, the expectations of conventional family life, and the moralism of the religious right. While their political involvement varies from group to group, their convictions are expressed in the belief that America was established "with liberty and justice for all."

As Wuthnow indicates, the religious right and their counterpart, the secular humanists and the religious left, are engaged in battle over which basic beliefs should govern our country. Both appeal to the American tradition, symbolized by the Pledge of Allegiance. One group's appeal is to "one nation under God"; the other's is to "liberty and justice for all." What have been called "mainline" churches find themselves caught in the middle of this battle over ideals.

The Episcopal Church stands within this middle group along with other denominations such as Lutheran, United Methodist, Presbyterian, Congregational (now the United Church of Christ), and Roman Catholic. The problem these denominations all confront is that they have some members who are in agreement with the religious right and others who side with the secular and religious left. Membership as a whole is clearly neither one nor the other, but both. Even within a single congregation, people who sit next to each other in worship may disagree hotly over particular issues.

On every issue that touches the family—abortion, sexual relations apart from marriage, homosexuality, women's roles—members of the mainline churches are divided. On political issues like the right to privacy, affirmative action, freedom of association, national health care, and covert military actions, the differences of opinion are equally great. To acknowledge these disagreements and to begin discussions in the church is, at least initially, to threaten to break the church apart. Members within the church are likely to see themselves not as struggling for the soul of America, but as struggling to save the soul of the church. Instead of a diverse, catholic community—catholic in the sense of universal, of embracing all peoples—the church is likely to become increasingly fragmented into congregations as people choose to join communities of like-minded souls. The danger is that instead of identifying with a larger church beyond the individual congregation, these congregations will see themselves *as* the church. They will identify with the left or the right or, alternatively, withdraw into an isolated religious sphere.

This sectarian impulse away from a catholic church is most apparent in the church's way of doing business, which is similar to that of political parties. People seek election and are elected to representative bodies of the church such as diocesan conventions and General Convention on the strength of their partisan views. Just as in secular government, interest groups lobby for the national church to take specific stances and adopt particular programs, while dioceses who disagree with these stances and programs withdraw their financial support. In this context, there seems to be no answer to the question, "How can we address issues of difference without splitting the church apart?" It seems that this split can only be avoided if Christian faith is not identified with particular decisions, judgments, and causes.

Again, sociologists are helpful in illuminating the social realities that reflect a larger and more catholic understanding of the church. In *American Mainline Religion*,[2] Wade Clarke Roof and William McKinney indicate two factors that explain why individuals commit themselves to a church. The first factor is a sense of belonging; people may identify with a church because it provides care and emotional support for them. More broadly, the church may be a primary social community, an extended family of sorts that lives and plays together. The second factor important for identifying with a church is the sense of meaning it provides, the fact that it helps people to make connections. Men and women may identify with a church because its activities and rituals give meaning and significance to the events of daily life. Worship, preaching, educational programs, retreats, meditations, and discussions are the reasons why people attend and support a church.

These two factors, belonging and meaning, reflect the traditional sociology of religious groups as studied by scholars like Ernest Troeltsch and H. Richard Niebuhr.[3] For people who perceive themselves as marginal to the society at large, the church functions as an alternative society by fulfilling the range of needs that are essential in human society, from personal acceptance and support to opportunities for exercising leadership and receiving respect and honor from peers. Where the church functions to meet such needs by being the primary social group for the individual, it becomes a sect in which belonging is all-important. By contrast, in churches where people do not see themselves as marginal but instead identify with the broader society, the church consecrates daily life in the social order by bestowing a larger sense of meaning and power. Here the church is not an alternative society; its members are equally citizens of the world. Meaning rather than belonging is what matters most.

Of course, the contrast between meaning and belonging is not as stark as this description suggests. No church or social organization can offer a sense of belonging without meaning, and shared meaning gives a sense of belonging together. I belong and, in this light, what is said in the context of my belonging is meaningful; because what is said is meaningful, I belong. But whether a church stresses belonging or meaning as primary does make a difference in its character.

Churches that emphasize belonging, such as the evangelical churches of the religious right, demand homogeneity and a certain sameness among their members. Members must share some basic attitudes and convictions in order to feel that they belong, and that is especially true when those in the society who hold divergent attitudes and beliefs are perceived as threatening or oppressive. Common beliefs bind a group together that feels marginal. In such churches clear teaching is emphasized; authority becomes concentrated in a single person or group of leaders who define acceptable beliefs. Among evangelical fundamentalists, for example, Scripture is a source but not the locus of authority. Authority belongs to a charismatic religious leader because he or she—usually he—is the one who interprets Scripture in order to define the literal meaning of the Bible. To disperse authority, and to allow and even embrace conflicting interpretations, is to undercut the homogeneity essential to a secure sense of belonging. The emphasis on belonging in church is, therefore, reflected in hierarchical forms of leadership or simply in autocratic leadership.

Churches that emphasize meaning over belonging do so because their members share a common understanding of Christian faith that informs but does not determine what ought to be done morally and politically. Individuals maintain their own identities and loyalties to other communities to which they belong. They identify with the church because it helps them to connect their lives with a sense of meaning and purpose that is broader than particular loyalties and judgments. The danger here is that worship and the church tend to become abstracted from daily life. Most commonly, worship becomes either a soothing mystery removed from the moral and political spheres altogether or a welcoming fellowship in which the notion of grace is reduced to a personal relationship with God.

In order to avoid religious abstraction or withdrawal from the world, teaching must take into account the diverse understandings within and without the church. Ambiguity and difference may not only be tolerated but accepted, as long as issues and questions are probed and insights are gained. Authority in such churches is dispersed among the members themselves. This is reflected for Protestants in an understanding of the priesthood of all believers; for Roman Catholics in the honoring of individual conscience; and for Anglicans in the conviction that the authority of teaching is based on the *consensus fidelium*, the sense or understanding shared in common by the faithful.

In this more catholic vision teaching is not a matter of setting down right belief. Rather, teaching is to present the understandings of the inherited tradition and the questions, challenges, and understandings that arise in the contemporary church and world. For example, since the early church first began to reflect on how Jesus reconciles humanity to God, there has not been a single understanding of Jesus' crucifixion. Some claim that Jesus is the perfect sacrifice that redeems the fallen order; others reject such a view of God and the cosmic order and instead understand the crucifixion as exemplary, as the example—in which we participate—of how our lives must be formed to be reconciled with God.[4] Teaching may then present the questions, challenges, and understandings of the present without demanding a narrow orthodoxy.

Whatever the issue, teaching seeks not conformity but understanding of what the witnesses have claimed in the past and what makes sense now. In most areas there will be some consensus on fundamental convictions. As grounded in Christian identity, Christians claim that Christ has transformed them, changed them in relationship to creation itself, given them new life. But transformation and new life do not mean uniformity of belief. How people are reconciled with God and what this means for our understanding of the world and for what we should do—such questioning stands at the heart of a serious engagement with the faith that has been given us. In more Protestant language, only in this way can the church proclaim and celebrate the gospel as a gospel of grace without identifying the gospel with a new law.

As the insights of sociology have shown, churches cannot address divisive issues through a narrowly legislative approach without dividing the church. In the Episcopal Church this too often happens, as each year diocesan conventions—and every three years, General Convention—are confronted by numerous resolutions. These may be described as memorials, legislative resolutions, and public declarations. While memorializing, legislating, and declaring its identity and stance is the task of a representative body, these resolutions have become a substitute for the task of teaching.

More specifically, memorials are resolutions that preserve our memory of a person, of specific work or service, or of an event. Like honorary degrees given by colleges and universities, memorials may serve other purposes, too—we might say the broader political purpose of gaining support. Whether seeking to set aside a day of celebration for the life and work of Martin Luther King, Jr., or thanking those who have provided leadership in the endowing of a retreat center, the essential purpose of a memorial is to express the general will of the church to celebrate what has been and to thank those who have served us all. How representative bodies address the question of memorials, moreover, points to the problem of simple democratic rule that makes teaching on the most fundamental and difficult issues impossible.

The outstanding question regarding memorials is not whether we should or shouldn't have them, but what process should be used in receiving, presenting, and deciding upon them. The potential for problems can be indicated by two questions. First, who formulates and presents memorials? And second, if everything is memorialized, what has really been memorialized? In other words, there must be both a process and a basis for identifying what is to be memorialized by the church if memorials are not to become either expressions of insignificant sentiments or public declarations that seek to define the church's will by the majority vote of representatives—whether in a congregation, diocese, or convention.

This question of the process by which to receive and decide upon memorials is part of the larger question of how to order the governance of the church in order to be a teaching church. We need a process that avoids unnecessary, divisive votes in which one side defines the identity of the church by a simple majority vote. Such votes are required where an issue—such as the ordination of women—is so central to people's understanding of Christian faith and life that it has to be resolved in order for people to decide whether to remain within the church or go their separate ways. But if the church is not to fall prey to the sectarian impulse, there must be no rush to judgment.

In contrast to memorials, legislative resolutions are those that direct the church—whether in congregations, dioceses, or at the national level—to undertake a specific action. These may include study, the development of teachings, change in policies, and the implementation of programs. A legislative resolution might direct a diocese to review parish assessments and make recommendations to ensure equity and participation, develop educational materials on human sexuality, or create a diocesan committee to make proposals for investing financially in local communities. Public declarations, on the other hand, are actions by convention that declare a public stance on specific issues that may include recommending particular actions to public officials. They speak to the larger society by addressing abortion or state lotteries or the use of military force.

Both legislative resolutions and public declarations arise out of specific concerns. The former arise when people seek changes in policy and organization or they want congregations, dioceses, or the national church to undertake specific actions; the latter come into being when people want to influence the world in which we live. Some legislative resolutions come directly from representative bodies and address areas about which they have knowledge and over which they have oversight. An example of this would be a resolution from the Commission on Ministry seeking a change in the national canons regarding procedures for ordination, such as reducing the number of psychiatric examinations from two to one. More difficult to address are resolutions raising issues or making specific proposals that do not themselves arise out of any broader work or teaching of the church. Such resolutions—perhaps focusing on scriptural authority, evangelism, sexual exploitation, or abortion—need to be addressed differently from those arising from the ongoing work of the councils of the church.

Rather than acting upon resolutions that come from an individual or particular group, resolutions that make particular prescriptions about the beliefs, order, and discipline of the church might be better referred to a representative body. Where specific actions are called for, a diocesan council could make decisions in light of broader considerations of issues, priorities, and strategies. Often, for example, a resolution calls for studying a controversial issue and then reporting back to the next convention. In itself, this defers action and suggests that something is being done, but nothing is really accomplished unless teachings are developed with an educational design that enables people to engage them. This cannot be done by a legislative body acting in a vacuum; the development of teaching, educational design, and materials requires resources. Even so, the outcome is likely to be inadequate unless there is some clarity about the purpose of teaching in the church.

Public declarations, no less than legislative resolutions, indicate areas of concern and conviction as people struggle to live out their Christian faith in the world. They differ in that they are addressed to public officials in order to determine or influence public policy. The church, if you will, seeks through public declarations to be the soul of the nation. These declarations, however, raise similar questions. Who speaks for the church? Does a resolution arise from a common mind informed by teaching in the church? Alternatively, does a resolution arise from a particular person or group?

Where a resolution expresses the mind of the church, it may be extremely appropriate for a convention to speak with one voice as a witness of faith. The power of such public declarations is that discussions have been broad; thus informed, the church has a clear stance and not simply a majority opinion. The stance of the church against apartheid in South Africa or segregation in this country are both examples of public declarations that for those in the church appear to be demanded by Christian faith itself. If taken seriously, such public declarations are a means of defining the faith and of drawing a line between what is acceptable and what is not, both morally and politically.

The difficulty regarding public declarations is that they often take a stance on issues about which there is no consensus within the church. While everyone presumably deplores poverty, the violent use of force, and drug abuse, agreement about how to address such evils is difficult. Since a specific policy may realize one set of goods only at the expense of others, public policies require judgments about the likely success of programs, decisions about priorities given limited resources, and compromises. Where there are disagreements about policies, resolutions fail. To the extent that they are perceived to represent only a particular group within the church, they are ignored from the outside. Within the church such public declarations are also ignored; they may even be damaging in cases where those who disagree with them are judged by the majority to be outside the community of faith.

When public declarations are passed and promulgated by the church, the sense of judgment and exclusion will increase if the declarations are not part of a broader and more comprehensive discussion and strategy for addressing a variety of issues that are of concern to members of the church. For example, for the church only to address a particular kind of issue—such as domestic and family issues or social justice and the structures of injustice—may well be experienced by those with different priorities as a judgment against them. Again, as with legislative resolutions, public declarations can only effectively express the witness of the community when they arise from broader discussions and a more comprehensive set of teachings.

What are the issues that the church should address? Why are they important for Christians? How have these issues been understood and addressed? What are the outstanding questions that we must now address? What then are the range of faithful responses, at least as far as we can discern? These are the questions that the church needs to answer. As the moral issues of homosexuality, abortion, and the use of military force painfully illustrate, there are a number of moral and political issues about which faithful people disagree. Rather than providing knowledgeable judgments, resolutions prescribe conclusions and draw lines that exclude those who disagree.

In addressing resolutions, the church must first listen and provide the opportunity to give voice to the concerns that stand behind particular resolutions and declarations. Second, resolutions that arise from the representative councils of the church need discussion and action so that the work of the church may proceed. Third, in cases where differences of opinion arise and teachings are lacking, these resolutions should not be voted upon. Whether they are legislative resolutions directed to the church or public declarations directed to the world, these resolutions must be tabled in order to develop teachings that inform decision-making and do not define Christian faith in narrow sectarian terms.

The way in which the church addresses resolutions reflects and influences the broader understanding of the nature of the church and Christian faith itself. As Episcopalians, catholic and reformed, we are formed as a community in which faith itself is not identified with singular dogmatic claims or particular moral prescriptions or policies. Rather, we are a diverse community, a catholic community, in which faithful people must struggle with theological and moral issues but may differ in understandings of those issues and in what it means to be faithful.

Teaching in the church is not a matter of advocating one position over another, but of informing understandings of faith and particular issues of concern. In this sense, teaching must articulate outstanding questions and issues before the church, provide an account of what the church has said and why, identify points of agreement, and critically explore and assess differences.

The Episcopal Church has failed to develop such teaching documents. In the Episcopal Church there are simply no teachings from the House of Bishops on major issues that confront the church, such as its understanding of ministry and holy orders, the nature of evangelism and Christian servanthood, or human sexuality and homosexuality. Instead, since it only voices conflicting claims, the church fails to mediate a coherent understanding of Christian faith that is convincing to individual members and effects a deeper identity and fidelity to that faith.

In light of his study of the social teachings of the church, Robert Hood concluded,

> There is no responsible or conscious effort to reflect theologically or historically on previous letters, resolutions, memorials, or policy statements.... The unsystematic, *ad hoc* character of the pronouncements allows for trendiness and single-issue oriented rather than considered thought.... [5]

What is needed are teachings that articulate a normative understanding of Christian faith and the Christian life that will enable individuals to form their lives and deepen their own faith. Resolutions, pastoral letters, and other teaching materials have failed to state what is central to Christian faith because they have lacked clarity about who they speak for, to whom they are addressed, and why an issue is important in terms of Christian faith. Such clarity may be gained by addressing the question, "Who is speaking to whom on what issues in what language and why?"[6]

The first question to be asked in order to develop or assess a teaching document is, "Who is speaking?" Is it the church as a communion of faithful persons, a group of theologians in the church, bishops in light of their own convictions, a representative body such as a church convention, or a prophetic minority? If authority rests on the consensus of the faithful, who could legitimately speak of that consensus? And even where there is a consensus, teaching requires some understanding of the legitimacy of dissent. Who can disagree and on what basis?

Second, in developing teachings the question needs to be asked, "Who is the audience? To whom is the document addressed?" Often the church is addressing the society at large in its pronouncements, as when speaking on nuclear disarmament or on the legality of abortion. This may be appropriate given the dual citizenship of Christians in the church and in the world; however, exclusive attention to the world prevents them from addressing the distinctive claims on Christians that arise from their Christian faith. The teachings of the church must arise from an identity that is grounded in the church; it cannot legitimately address the world until it addresses the church. Christians must first of all be clear why they should be concerned about a specific issue, what challenges it raises, and what have been the range of responses.

In terms of moral teaching, Christians may have distinctive reasons for addressing and responding to issues such as respect for life, stewardship, vocation, friendship and service, the family, justice, the use of violence, and the economy. They should, therefore, choose the language they use to reflect these distinctive reasons. For example, Christians may feel compelled to respond to the homeless out of their understanding of the reign of God, of covenant and fidelity, of imitation and discipleship, of the mission of the church, of the command of God, or of the Trinitarian God as creator, redeemer, and sanctifier. Inadequate attention to the use of language arises in part from lack of clarity about authorship and audience, about who is speaking to whom. The failure to develop a language that will express what is central to Christian faith, however, also reflects the lack of a coherent understanding of Christian faith itself.

Responsibility for addressing the crisis in governance and teaching finally rests with the bishops of the church. As expressed in their ordination vows, in assuming pastoral oversight over the community of faith bishops are given the authority "to guard the faith, unity, and discipline of the Church" (BCP, 517). This is not to suggest that bishops alone should speak for the church nor that a single structure and form is needed or able to address outstanding issues.

Instead, teachings may be developed in a variety of ways. For example, bishops may assume direct responsibility for writing teachings, as in the case of pastoral letters or what have been called pastoral teachings. A model for such teachings are provided by the National Conference of Catholic Bishops in the writing of their pastoral letters on peace and on the economy. The structure of the national church could also provide a means of drawing together people to develop teaching materials. These teachings may reflect a particular point of view while acknowledging other positions and points of view, which is how the Evangelical Lutheran Church in America has developed its teaching on homosexuality. The General Synod Board for Social Responsibility in the Church of England has similarly written a range of teaching materials. Furthermore, individual dioceses might undertake their own resources for teaching, as did the Episcopal Diocese of Washington in its study of nuclear deterrence. Individual writings, including those by seminary faculty and others trained in theological studies, are also important if the church is to have a broad base of teachings that inform individual understandings while reflecting different concerns and perspectives.[7]

Dispersed authority and teachings, however, requires some oversight in order to focus the resources necessary for writing, publication, and distribution of educational materials that make such teachings available. These are major needs that are difficult to address adequately. For example, in developing teachings from the bishops themselves, administrative oversight requires someone with an understanding of the needs and problems in governance and teaching for the church, including the political *savoir faire* to effect a process that will not be dominated by the particular interests of any one group. In terms of teachings, the resources needed are numerous, varied, and broad, providing a whole spectrum of conflicting interpretations and prescriptions. Understanding an issue requires the perspectives from a range of theological personnel (including biblical scholars, historians, theologians, and ethicists), from people entirely outside of religious studies (including historians, social scientists, and public policy planners), and from those who have come up against these issues in their own personal lives. Finally, making teaching material available includes distribution, the development of secondary materials like teaching guides, and the training of the teachers themselves.

To write, publish, and disseminate teachings from the bishops or from the national church will require significant appropriations in the national church budget and thereby an assessment and change in the structure and deployment of professional resources. This is made more difficult by the claims on available funds by a range of particular interest groups and by a bureaucracy which has developed constituencies whom the professional personnel serve. The changes necessary to develop and support adequately the bishops and the church in its teaching are politically difficult, and such support can only come about if there is broad consensus among the bishops about the gravity of the crisis.

According to the *Oxford English Dictionary*, piety is "the habitual reference and obedience to God, the faithfulness to parents, family and our superiors, or religious devotion."[8] Piety is not a narrow matter of the heart, but of the whole person. It refers not only to dispositions but to intentions and actions as well. In piety all things are referred to God. In this sense piety is a way of life; Christian piety is a way of life given and formed in Jesus Christ.

Reverence and fidelity indicate the double movement of piety. Reverence points to religious devotion, the purpose of which is to bring us into the presence of God. Corporate worship and private prayer vary, but they have the common purpose of enabling our participation in the story of Christ. More specifically, in telling and connecting the Christian story to our lives, worship removes our preoccupations, dispossesses us, and brings us into the presence of God so that we may acknowledge God as God. In this way reverence as piety is marked by awe, dependence, and thanksgiving. In turn, reverence is inseparable from fidelity, from living out the story of Christ in our lives. Leading to and arising from the experience of the presence of God, Christians bear witness to God in their lives by sharing the story of Christ and living that story in the world.

As the two basic sacraments of the Christian life, baptism and eucharist celebrate this twofold movement of faith. In reenacting Jesus' own offering of himself, baptism brings us into the presence of God as we confess what this requires in our life as members of the church and citizens of the world. The eucharist celebrates this identity in our ongoing life. Together these two primary sacraments of the church make clear that our life in God—a life transformed, given new birth, reconciled, liberated, empowered—is a life offered with Christ in thanksgiving to God. And this offering is never simply a matter of religious devotion. It is always a way of life marked by repentance and forgiveness, praise and thanksgiving, compassion and hospitality. This way of life may be described as a life of service or servanthood, but only when service is tied to evangelism. Christians do not act to bring in the reign of God, to make God present, but share in Christ's life as disciples of Christ who are living in God's reign. Their lives are signs of God's presence among us as revealed in Christ.

Deeds then require implicit if not explicit interpretation: as disciples Christians are called to proclaim the story of Christ. In this proclamation Christians seek to give voice to who the person of Christ is, what is finally revealed, and what is required. Such articulations and practical guidance, however, are never a substitute for piety itself. Reverence and fidelity arise from a person and not an idea. The danger of substituting the idea for the reality, however, is always present, especially given the human hope to have resurrection and new life apart from suffering and, ultimately, crucifixion. In this sense, it is idolatrous to identify faith with purity of belief or practice.

The politics of the church need to serve true piety. This requires ordering the resources of the church for discipleship, while preventing the power of particular experiences and convictions from too narrowly defining Christian faith and thereby dividing the church. The politics of piety must not itself be governed by the sectarian impulse.

Endnotes

1. Robert Wuthnow, *The Struggle for America's Soul* (Grand Rapids, MI: Eerdmans, 1989).

2. Clarke Wade Roof and William McKinney, *American Mainline Religion* (New Brunswick, NJ: Rutgers, 1987).

3. The classic study remains Ernest Troeltsch, *The Social Teaching of the Christian Churches*, 2 vols. (Louisville, KY: Westminster/John Knox, 1992; 1st German ed. 1912). In the United States, see H. Richard Niebuhr, *The Social Sources of Denominationalism* (New York: Henry Holt, 1929) and *The Kingdom of God in America* (New York: Harper and Row, 1937).

4. See David H. Smith, "Suffering, Medicine, and Christian Theology," *On Moral Medicine*, Stephen E. Lammers and Allen Verhey, eds. (Grand Rapids, MI: Eerdmans, 1987), pp. 255- 261.

5. Robert E. Hood, "Does the Episcopal Church Have Social Teachings?" in *Anglican Theological Review* LXX (January 1988), 1:83. See also Robert Hood, *Social Teachings of the Episcopal Church* (Harrisburg, PA: Morehouse, 1990), and Timothy F. Sedgwick and Philip Turner, eds., *The Crisis in Moral Teaching in the Episcopal Church* (Harrisburg, PA: Morehouse, 1992). For reflection on the task and

problems of moral teaching in the Church of England, see Church of England Board for Social Responsibility, *The Church of England and Politics* (Cowley, Oxford: Bocardo & Church Army Press, 1980), esp. pp. 81-117.

6. See *The Crisis in Moral Teaching in the Episcopal Church*, especially Philip Turner, "How the Church Might Teach," pp. 137-159.

7. See National Conference of Catholic Bishops, *The Challenge of Peace* (Washington, D.C.: United States Catholic Conference, 1983), and *Economic Justice for All* (Washington, D.C.: United States Catholic Conference, 1986); Lutheran Church in America, *A Study of Issues Concerning Homosexuality* (Division of Missions, 1986; available from the Evangelical Lutheran Church in America, 8765 W. Higgins Road, Chicago, IL 60631); the Church of England Board for Social Responsibility, *Prisons and Prisoners in England Today* (London: Church Information Office, 1978), *Homosexual Relations* (London: Church Information Office, 1979), and *The Church and the Bomb: Nuclear Weapons and Christian Conscience* (London: Church Information Office and Hodder and Stoughton, 1982); the Episcopal Diocese of Washington, *The Nuclear Dilemma: A Christian Search for Understanding* (Cincinnati, OH: Forward Movement, 1987).

8. *The Oxford English Dictionary*, vol. 7 (Oxford: Clarendon, 1933), p. 843.

Afterword

These chapters draw selectively from a variety of lectures and presentations that I have been asked to give, and some of these have found their way into publication. Through the Council for the Development of Ministry (CDM), the Commissions on Ministry from the dioceses of Province III invited me in 1986 to propose theological criteria for the selection of persons for holy orders. The manuscript for that occasion, "On Theology, Ministry, and Holy Orders," was then distributed to the House of Bishops and chairs of diocesan Commissions on Ministry and published in the April 1987 issue of the *Anglican Theological Review*.

The chapter on Anglican identity is drawn in part from a lecture given in 1987 at the invitation of the School of Theology at the University of the South in Sewanee, and later published in *St. Luke's Journal of Theology*. Similarly, the Diocese of Chicago helped my reflections on lay ministry by asking me to lead a lay ministries day in 1988; the keynote address, "Making the Connections: Developing the Ministry of the Laity," was later published in the Episcopal Church's *Ministry Development Journal*.

Invitations by the dioceses of Minnesota and Michigan to speak to their diocesan conventions in 1990 and 1992 enabled me to develop further my reflections on the crisis confronting the church. A consultation of Anglican ethicists on the task of the church in its teaching met from 1987 to 1989, and from this work two publications appeared from which I have drawn here. The presentation to the diocese of Minnesota was published in 1991 by Forward Movement as "Dealing with Differences in Councils and Conventions of the Church," while "The Crisis of Authority and the Need for an Ecclesial Ethic" appeared in the *Anglican Theological Review* (January 1990).

Finally, the chapter on clergy ethics is a revised version of "An Outline for a Clergy Ethic," which came out of my experiences conducting clergy conferences in the dioceses of Minnesota and Southern Ohio in 1991. This was published in *Sewanee Theological Review* (Winter 1991).

Other opportunities have also informed my thought and have furthered the development of the larger argument here. These include the Pan-Anglican Symposium on Mission in Hong Kong in 1986; the opportunity to offer two lectures on the mission of the church and the ordering of ministry for the diocese of Arizona in 1987; a paper on the nature of mission as part of a 1987 consultation on the House of Bishops' proposed pastoral letter on ministry; two keynote addresses in 1987 on the cathedral and the mission of the church for the North American Conference of Deans; and a lecture and presentation for long-range planning at St. Paul's Church in Indianapolis in 1991.